Pensions at a Glance
Asia/Pacific
2018

This work is published under the responsibility of the Secretary-General of the OECD. The opinions expressed and arguments employed herein do not necessarily reflect the official views of OECD member countries.

This document, as well as any data and any map included herein, are without prejudice to the status of or sovereignty over any territory, to the delimitation of international frontiers and boundaries and to the name of any territory, city or area.

Please cite this publication as:
OECD (2018), *Pensions at a Glance Asia/Pacific 2018*, OECD Publishing, Paris.
https://doi.org/10.1787/pension_asia-2018-en

ISBN 978-92-64-30868-8 (print)
ISBN 978-92-64-30869-5 (pdf)

Annual: Pensions at a Glance Asia/Pacific
ISSN 2309-0758 (print)
ISSN 2309-0766 (online)

The statistical data for Israel are supplied by and under the responsibility of the relevant Israeli authorities. The use of such data by the OECD is without prejudice to the status of the Golan Heights, East Jerusalem and Israeli settlements in the West Bank under the terms of international law.

Corrigenda to OECD publications may be found on line at: *www.oecd.org/publishing/corrigenda*.
© OECD 2018

You can copy, download or print OECD content for your own use, and you can include excerpts from OECD publications, databases and multimedia products in your own documents, presentations, blogs, websites and teaching materials, provided that suitable acknowledgement of OECD as source and copyright owner is given. All requests for public or commercial use and translation rights should be submitted to *rights@oecd.org*. Requests for permission to photocopy portions of this material for public or commercial use shall be addressed directly to the Copyright Clearance Center (CCC) at *info@copyright.com* or the Centre français d'exploitation du droit de copie (CFC) at *contact@cfcopies.com*.

Foreword

This study presents a range of indicators to enable comparisons between the pension systems of economies in the Asia/Pacific region. It also includes data for key countries that are members of the Organisation for Economic Co-operation and Development (OECD). It builds on the first *Pensions at a Glance: Asia/Pacific* which was also a joint project between the World Bank and the OECD, along with the OECD/Government of Korea Research Centre on Health and Social Policies (RCHSP) and updates the 2013 edition.

This report was prepared, under the general supervision of Gabriela Ramos, OECD Chief of Staff and Sherpa to the G20. The report was drafted by Andrew Reilly of the Social Policy Division of the OECD Secretariat and benefited from extensive comments by both Hervé Boulhol, Head of the Pension Team and Monika Queisser, Head of the Social Policy Division. Lucy Hulett prepared the manuscript for publication.

For this fourth report we are again indebted to the national experts who have contributed to the updating of the models used, many of whom also assisted with the first two publications. They are too numerous to mention here but details of attendees to the annual pension meetings in Seoul can be found on the Korea Centre website www.oecdkorea.org/social/board/list_eng.asp?BoardCd=5011. We are also indebted to the Korea Centre for all their assistance in organising the annual meetings and for coordinating contacts with national experts.

Table of contents

Foreword 3

Executive Summary 7

Chapter 1. Design of pension systems 9
    Architecture of national pension systems 10
    Basic, targeted and minimum pensions 12
    Mandatory earnings-related pensions 14
    Retirement ages 16

Chapter 2. Retirement-income indicators 19
    Methodology and assumptions 20
    Gross replacement rates 22
    Net replacement rates 24
    Gross pension wealth 26
    Net pension wealth 28
    Pension earnings link 30
    Coverage 32
    Life expectancy 34
    Support ratio 36

Chapter 3. Pensions at a Glance Asia/Pacific: Pension profiles 39
    Introduction 40
    China 41
    Hong Kong, China 44
    India 47
    Indonesia 52
    Malaysia 55
    Pakistan 58
    Philippines 61
    Singapore 64
    Sri Lanka 69
    Thailand 72
    Viet Nam 75

Tables

Table 1.1. Structure of future mandatory retirement-income provision 11
Table 1.2. Basic, targeted and minimum pensions, 2016 13
Table 1.3. Average annual earnings 13
Table 1.4. Future parameters and rules of mandatory earnings-related pensions 15

Table 1.5. Early and normal retirement ages for an individual entering the labour market or retiring in 2016 by type of pension scheme 17
Table 2.1. Gross pension replacement rates by earnings, men and women 23
Table 2.2. Net pension replacement rates by earnings, men and women.. 25
Table 2.3. Gross pension wealth by earnings, men and women.. 27
Table 2.4. Net pension wealth by earnings, men and women 29
Table 2.5. Membership of mandatory pension schemes by population and labour force 33

Figures

Figure 1.1. Taxonomy: Different types of retirement-income provision 11
Figure 2.1. Gross pension replacement rates by earnings, low and average earners............................ 23
Figure 2.2. Net pension replacement rates by earnings, low and average earners 25
Figure 2.3. Gross pension wealth by earnings, low and average earners 27
Figure 2.4. Net pension wealth by earnings, low and average earners... 29
Figure 2.5. The link between pre-retirement earnings and pension entitlements................................. 31
Figure 2.6. Coverage of mandatory pension schemes by population and labour force........................ 33
Figure 2.7. Life expectancy at birth, in years, men and women, 2015-20 35
Figure 2.8. Life expectancy at age 65, in years, men and women, 2015-20 and 2060-65 35
Figure 2.9. Old-age support ratio, 2015 and 2055.. 37
Figure 2.10. Old-age population projections.. 37

Follow OECD Publications on:

 http://twitter.com/OECD_Pubs

 http://www.facebook.com/OECDPublications

 http://www.linkedin.com/groups/OECD-Publications-4645871

 http://www.youtube.com/oecdilibrary

 http://www.oecd.org/oecddirect/

This book has...
A service that delivers Excel® files from the printed page!

Look for the *StatLinks* at the bottom of the tables or graphs in this book. To download the matching Excel® spreadsheet, just type the link into your Internet browser, starting with the *http://dx.doi.org* prefix, or click on the link from the e-book edition.

Executive Summary

The biggest challenges facing pension systems in non-OECD Asian economies are rapid population ageing and low coverage, both for those receiving benefits and those contributing to the pension systems. Efforts to close the coverage gap by expanding eligibility to larger shares of the labour force or through non-contributory pensions are at the heart of most discussions. Increasing life expectancy will jeopardise financial sustainability as people live longer in retirement and the number of pensioners relative to contributors grows. However, as in other regions, pension reform is politically challenging as is often entails unpopular measures, such as increasing the retirement age, lowering benefits or increasing contribution rates.

The international exchange of pension reform approaches and experiences can provide valuable lessons for the design and implementation of future reforms. However, it is not always easy to compare the functioning of national pension systems, due to significant differences in institutional, technical, and legal details.

This study combines rigorous analysis with clear, easy-to-understand presentation of empirical results. It does not advocate any particular kind of pension system or type of reform. The goal is to inform debates on retirement-income systems with data that policy-makers, experts and stakeholders with different visions for the future of pensions can all use as a reference point.

The format of this fourth report follows that of the previous editions which were based on the OECD's Pensions at a Glance series covering the 36 OECD member countries. The values contained within reflect the pension parameters in 2016. As with the original publications the report refers to single pensioners rather than family units.

The results are specifically analysed at three distinct earnings levels so that a more comprehensive portrayal of the individual pension systems is given. Firstly, results are given for workers at average earnings, where it is assumed that the worker earns this level throughout their entire career without any period of interruption. The remaining two earnings levels are 50% of average earnings, commonly called low earners, and 200% of average earnings, referred to as high earners. These earnings levels apply to the entire working life of the individual. Entry to the pension system is assumed to be at age 20 and the models are based on a full career until the normal retirement age within that economy, so for China, for example, it is assumed that a man will have to work for 40 years until age 60 before being eligible for retirement pension.

The report begins by showing the different schemes that make up each national retirement-income provision, including a summary of the rules that apply. This is then followed by a brief summary of several indicators that are the benchmarks of any pension system analysis, namely replacement rates and pension wealth. These indicators are examined on both a gross and net basis. The subsequent sections then look further at both the characteristics of Asian pension systems as well as the population as a whole, through coverage, life expectancy and general demographics. Finally Chapter 3 of the report provides detailed background information for all of the non-OECD economies covered. Information on the OECD countries is available online in the Pensions at a Glance series at http://oe.cd/pag.

In order to enable comparison between the non-OECD economies and specific OECD countries the results have been grouped by region and OECD status. The largest such grouping is East Asia/Pacific which covers China, Hong Kong, China, Indonesia, Malaysia, the Philippines, Singapore, Thailand and Viet Nam. Within South Asia the remaining non-OECD economies are listed, i.e. India, Pakistan and Sri Lanka. Furthermore the OECD countries themselves have been divided into two distinct groups. Firstly, there are the Asia/Pacific economies of Australia, Canada, Japan, Korea, New Zealand and the United States to enable a more regional comparison. Secondly, four additional OECD countries are included, France, Germany, Italy and the United Kingdom, all of which have well established pension systems and are major economic powers. By including this latter group clear differences should be evident between them and the non-OECD economies in Asia.

Chapter 1. Design of pension systems

The five indicators in this section look in detail at the design of national retirement income systems in the economies under study. The first indicator sets out the taxonomy of the different kinds of retirement-income programmes found around the world. It uses this framework to describe the architecture of the 11 economies' pension systems.

The next three indicators set out the parameters and rules of the pension systems. The description begins with second indicator covering basic, targeted and minimum income systems, showing the values of these systems. The third indicator looks at the mandatory earnings-related pensions systems. It shows how benefits are determined in these schemes and the range of earnings that are covered. The fourth indicator presents the current and future retirement ages by pension scheme for individuals. Current age are for those who retired in 2016 after a full career from age 20, whilst future ages are the future retirement ages for an individual entering the labour market at age 20 in 2016.

Architecture of national pension systems

> **Key results**
>
> Retirement-income regimes are diverse and often involve a number of different programmes. Classifying pension systems and different retirement-income schemes is consequently difficult. The taxonomy of pensions used here consists of two mandatory "tiers": an adequacy part and an earnings-related part. Voluntary provision, be it individual or employer-provided, makes up a third tier.

The framework, shown in the chart, is based on the role and objective of each part of the system. The first tier comprises programmes designed to ensure pensioners achieve some absolute, minimum standard of living. The second-tier, earnings-related components, are designed to achieve some target standard of living in retirement compared with that when working. Within these tiers, schemes are classified further by provider (public or private) and the way benefits are determined. Pensions at a Glance focuses mainly on these mandatory components although information is also provided on some voluntary, private schemes.

Using this framework, the architecture of national schemes is shown in the table. Programmes aimed to prevent poverty in old age – first-tier schemes – are provided by the public sector and are of three main types.

Basic pensions can take two different forms: a benefit paid to everyone irrespective of any contributions made, although beneficiaries might have to meet some residence criteria. In some economies residence-based benefits are potentially offset against other pension income; or a benefit paid solely on the basis of the number of years of contributions, i.e. independently of earnings. Only two Asian economies have a basic pension scheme or other provisions with a similar effect.

Minimum pensions can refer to either the minimum of a specific contributory scheme or of all schemes combined. They are found in five Asian economies. The value of entitlements takes account only of pension income: unlike means-tested schemes, it is not affected by income from savings, etc.

Social assistance plans pay a higher benefit to poorer pensioners and reduced benefits to better-off retirees. In these plans, the value of the benefit depends either on income from other sources or on both income and assets. Most economies have general social safety-nets of this type.

Defined benefit (DB) plans are provided by the public sector in five economies. Retirement income depends on the number of years of contributions and individual earnings.

Defined contribution (DC) plans are compulsory in seven economies. In these schemes, contributions flow into an individual account. The accumulation of contributions and investment returns is usually converted into a pension-income stream at retirement.

Within the OECD countries shown there are two additional schemes. First, in *points* schemes workers earn pension points based on their earnings each year. At retirement, the sum of pension points is multiplied by a pension-point value to convert them into a regular pension payment. Second, *notional-accounts* schemes record contributions in an individual account and apply a rate of return to the balances. The accounts are "notional" in that the balances exist only on the books of the managing institution. At retirement, the accumulated notional capital is converted into a stream of pension payments using a formula based on life expectancy. Since this is designed to mimic DC schemes, they are often called notional defined contribution plans (NDC).

1. DESIGN OF PENSION SYSTEMS

Figure 1.1. Taxonomy: Different types of retirement-income provision

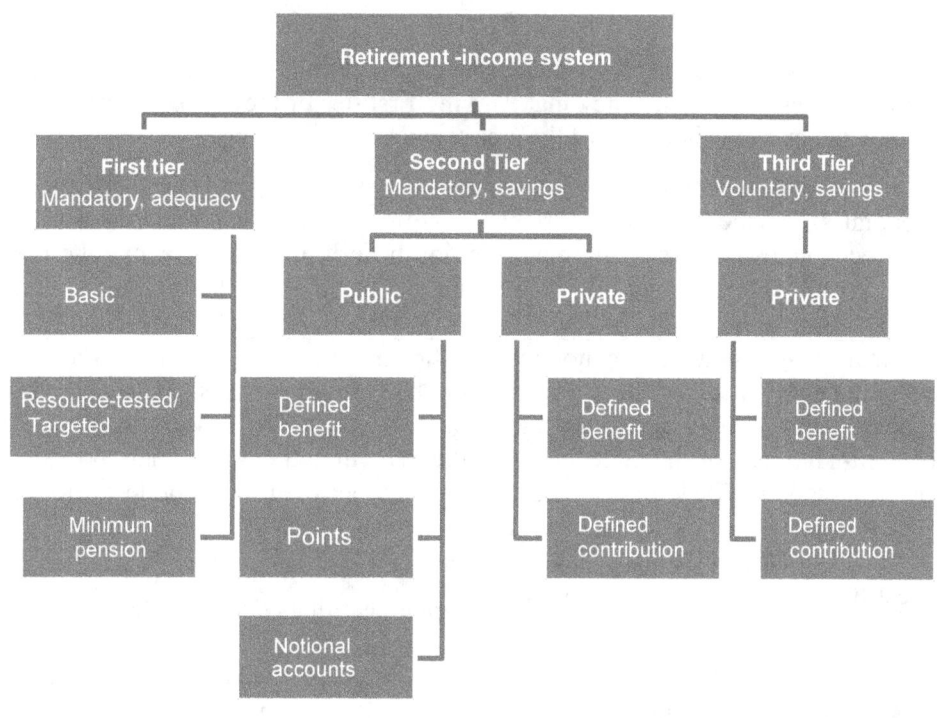

Table 1.1. Structure of future mandatory retirement-income provision

	Basic	Minimum	Social assistance	Public Type	Private Type		Basic	Minimum	Social assistance	Public Type	Private Type
East Asia/Pacific						**OECD Asia/Pacific**					
China					DC	Australia	✓				DC
Hong Kong, China	✓		✓		DC	Canada	✓		✓	DB	
Indonesia		✓			DC	Japan	✓			DB	
Malaysia			✓		DC	Korea			✓	DB	
Philippines	✓	✓		DB		New Zealand	✓				
Singapore					DC	United States				DB	
Thailand			✓	DB							
Viet Nam		✓	✓	DB		**Other OECD**					
						France			✓	DB+Points	
South Asia						Germany				Points	
India		✓	✓	DB/DC		Italy			✓	NDC	
Pakistan		✓		DB		United Kingdom	✓				
Sri Lanka					DC						

Note: DB = defined benefit; DC = defined contribution; NDC = notional accounts.
Source: See Chapter 3 for Asian economies and "Country Profiles" available at http://oe.cd/pag for OECD countries.

StatLink http://dx.doi.org/10.1787/888933873136

1. DESIGN OF PENSION SYSTEMS

Basic, targeted and minimum pensions

> **Key results**
>
> Basic and minimum pensions along with social assistance are defined as the first layer of protection for the elderly within the pension system. They make up the first tier of the taxonomy of pension systems, which was set out in the previous indicator of the architecture of national pension schemes.
>
> Basic pensions only exist in two non-OECD economies compared to five of the OECD countries listed. Five Asian economies provide a social assistance benefit equivalent to 8.1% of average earnings. Furthermore, five economies provide a minimum pension benefit, most often above the basic or social assistance level. For a full-career worker, the average minimum pension is 24.5% of average earnings.

There are three main ways in which economies might provide retirement incomes to meet a minimum standard of living in old age (Table 1.2). The left-hand part of the table shows the value of benefits provided under these different types of scheme. Values are presented in absolute terms – national currency units. They are also given in relative terms – as a percentage of economy-wide average earnings – to facilitate comparisons between economies.

Benefit values are shown for a single person. In some cases – usually with minimum contributory pensions – each partner in a couple receives an individual entitlement. In other cases – especially for targeted schemes – the couple is treated as the unit of assessment and generally receives less than twice the entitlement of a single person.

The analysis of benefit values can be complicated by the existence of multiple programmes in some economies. However, in non-OECD Asian economies this is very rarely the case as only India and Viet Nam have dual systems.

There are five economies that do not have either a basic or minimum pension within their system (China, Malaysia, Singapore, Sri Lanka and Thailand). Basic pensions exist in only Hong Kong, China and the Philippines, with the latter also having a minimum pension along with India, Indonesia, Pakistan and Viet Nam.

Table 1.4 reports the average wage (AW) levels for the year 2016. Average wages are displayed in national currencies and in US dollars (both at market exchange rates and at purchasing power parities, PPP). The PPP exchange rate adjusts for the fact that the purchasing power of a dollar varies between economies: it allows for differences in the price of a basket of goods and services between economies.

Wage earnings across the Asian economies averaged USD 9 660 in 2016 at market exchange rates. Singapore has the highest at USD 42 070, more than double the next highest in Hong Kong, China at USD 20 349 and nearly 30 times that recorded in Indonesia (USD 1 422).

At PPP wages averaged USD 20 432. Singapore is again highest amongst the Asian economies, at USD 70 800, with Malaysia next at USD 58 800. Indonesia is again the lowest at USD 4 692 but India Pakistan and the Philippines are also under USD 6 000. The higher figure for PPP wages suggests that many economies exchange rates with the US dollar were lower than the rate that would equalise the cost of a standard basket of goods and services.

Average wages for the OECD countries are much higher, averaging USD 36 622 at market exchange rates and USD 42 682 at PPP exchange rates. Australia has the highest wages at market exchange rates for those OECD countries listed at USD 59 134, with Germany highest at USD 61 451 for PPP rates, nearly USD 10 000 lower than that of Singapore.

Table 1.2. Basic, targeted and minimum pensions, 2016

	Relative benefit value (% of AW earnings)			Absolute value (units of national currency per year)				Relative benefit value (% of AW earnings)			Absolute value (units of national currency per year)		
	Basic	Minimum	Social assistance	Basic	Minimum	Social assistance		Basic	Minimum	Social assistance	Basic	Minimum	Social assistance
China	x	x	x	x	x	x	Australia	27.6	x	x	22 677	x	x
Hong Kong, China	9.8	x	19.0	15 480	x	29 940	Canada	13.5	x	19.2	6 879	x	9 803
India	x	12.1	2.4	x	12 000	2 400	Japan	15.3	x	19.0	780 100	x	970 380
Indonesia	x	12.3	x	x	3 600 000	x	Korea	x	x	5.5	x	x	2 400 000
Malaysia	x	x	4.3	x	x	3 600	New Zealand	40.0	x	x	23 058	x	x
Pakistan	x	39.3	x	x	63 000	x	United States	x	x	16.7	x	x	8 796
Philippines	3.4	27.5	x	3 900	31 200	x							
Singapore	x	x	x	x	x	x	France	x	21.7	25.3	x	8 256	9 610
Sri Lanka	x	x	x	x	x	x	Germany	x	x	20.1	x	x	9 588
Thailand	x	x	4.1	x	x	7 200	Italy	x	21.3	19.0	x	6 525	5 825
Viet Nam	x	31.5	10.5	x	14 520 000	4 860 000	United Kingdom	22.2	x	x	8 122	x	x

Note: x = Not applicable.

StatLink http://dx.doi.org/10.1787/888933873155

Table 1.3. Average annual earnings

	Average earnings			Exchange rates with USD	
Individual earnings (% average)	National currency	USD, market price	USD, PPP	Market price	PPPs
China	67 569	9 730	19 300	6.94	3.50
Hong Kong, China	157 800	20 349	27 254	7.75	5.79
Indonesia	19 200 000	1 422	4 692	13 499.50	4 091.831
Malaysia	83 496	18 613	58 800	4.49	1.42
Philippines	107 399	2 165	5 977	49.61	17.97
Singapore	60 888	42 070	70 800	1.45	0.86
Thailand	174 319	4 868	13 990	35.81	12.46
Viet Nam	46 100 000	2 025	6 096	22 769.00	7 562.94
India	99 349	1 462	5 665	67.97	17.54
Pakistan	160 280	1 537	5 579	104.30	28.73
Sri Lanka	300 000	2 021	6 595	148.44	45.49
Australia	82 114	59 134	56 016	1.39	1.47
Canada	50 997	37 935	40 181	1.34	1.27
Japan	5 110 601	43 692	50 086	116.97	102
Korea	43 857 243	36 328	49 071	1 207.26	894
New Zealand	57 649	39 912	39 756	1.44	1.45
United States	52 543	52 543	52 543	1.00	1.00
France	38 049	40 038	47 355	0.95	0.804
Germany	47 809	50 307	61 451	0.95	0.778
Italy	30 642	32 243	42 370	0.95	0.723
United Kingdom	36 571	45 100	52 731	0.81	0.694
OECD35		36 622	42 682		

Note: PPP = Purchasing Power Parity.
Source: OECD pension models.

StatLink http://dx.doi.org/10.1787/888933873174

Mandatory earnings-related pensions

> **Key results**
>
> The second-tier of the OECD's taxonomy of retirement-income provision comprises mandatory earnings-related pensions. Key parameters and rules of these schemes determine the value of entitlements, including the long-term effect of pension reforms that have already been legislated.

Earnings-related schemes can be of four different types: defined benefit (DB), points, notional defined contribution (NDC), or defined contribution (DC). The accrual rate shows the rate at which benefit entitlements build up for each year of coverage. The accrual rate is expressed as a percentage of the earnings that are "covered" by the pension scheme.

For points systems, the effective accrual rate is calculated as the ratio of the cost of a pension point to the pension-point value. In notional-accounts schemes, the effective accrual rate is calculated in a similar way; it depends on the contribution rate, notional interest rate and annuity factors. In Thailand and Viet Nam the accrual rates are not constant, in contrast to all the other economies that have DB systems. In Thailand the first 15 years of contribution give 20% with each subsequent year giving 1.5%. In Viet Nam the accrual rates have been different for men and women but these have being equalised from 2018.

Earnings measures used to calculate benefits also differ. Three economies solely use lifetime earnings to calculate benefits, China, Indonesia and Viet Nam, with the Philippines using the higher of lifetime earnings the final five years. Thailand also uses the final five years for the calculation of benefits whilst Pakistan just uses the last year of salary.

Closely linked with the earnings measure is valorisation, whereby past earnings are adjusted to take account of changes in "living standards" between the time pension rights accrued and the time they are claimed (sometimes called pre-retirement indexation). The uprating of the pension-point value and the notional interest rate in points and notional-accounts systems, respectively, are the exact corollaries of valorisation in DB plans. The most common practice is to revalue earlier years' pay with price inflation, used in four economies compared to the growth of average earnings, which is used in only two.

One key parameter for defined contribution (DC) plans is the proportion of earnings that must be paid into the individual account, as this is directly linked to size of the pension pot at retirement. Seven Asian economies have defined contribution systems and the average contribution rate is 17% across the economies, ranging from a high of 37% in Singapore to a low of 5.7% in Indonesia.

Some economies set a limit on the earnings used to calculate both contribution liabilities and pension benefits. The average ceiling on public pensions for the three economies is 175% of average economy-wide earnings, though this excludes the other eight economies that do not have a ceiling.

Indexation refers to the uprating of pensions in payment. Price indexation is most common, being applicable for three economies. Viet Nam uses wage indexation with both China and Thailand having a discretionary indexation to a combination of wages and prices.

Table 1.4. Future parameters and rules of mandatory earnings-related pensions

	DB, Points or NDC schemes					DC schemes	Ceilings on pensionable earnings (% of average earnings)	
	Type	Accrual rate (%)	Earnings measure	Valorisation	Indexation	Contribution rate (%)	Public	Private
East Asia/Pacific								
China	DB	1.00	L	w	d	8		
Hong Kong, China						10	228	
Indonesia	DB	1.00	L	p	p	5.7		
Malaysia						20-21		
Philippines	DB	2.00	max. (f5,L)	p	p			
Singapore	None					37	118	
Thailand	DB	1.33/1.5	f5	p	d			
Viet Nam	DB	2.0/3.0	L	w	w			
South Asia								
India	DB					15.67	181	
Pakistan	DB	2.00	f1	p	p			
Sri Lanka	None					20		
OECD Asia/Pacific								
Australia	None					9.5-12		248
Canada	DB	0.64	L(83%b)	w	p [c]		108	
Japan	DB	0.55	L	w	w/p		234	
Korea	DB	1.00	L	w	p		119	
New Zealand	None							
United States	DB	0.75[w]	b35	w	p		226	
Other OECD								
France	DB/points	1.12	b25/L	p/p	p/p		0	
Germany	Points	1.00	L	w [c]	w [c]		156	
Italy	NDC	1.46	L	GDP	p		327	
United Kingdom	None							

Note: Parameters are for 2016 but include all legislated changes that take effect in the future: for example, some economies are extending the period of earnings covered for calculating benefits. Empty cells indicate that the parameter is not relevant. [a] =Varies with age; [b] = Number of best years; [c] = Valorisation/indexation conditional on financial sustainability; [d] = Discretionary indexation; DB = Defined benefit; DC =Defined contribution; f = Number of final years; fr = Fixed rate valorisation; GDP = Growth of gross domestic product; L = Lifetime average; NDC = Nonfinancial accounts; p = Valorisation/indexation with prices; w = Valorisation/indexation with average earnings; [w] = Varies with earnings; [y] = Varies with years of service.

StatLink http://dx.doi.org/10.1787/888933873193

Retirement ages

> The rules for eligibility to retire and withdraw a pension benefit are complex and often reflect conflicting objectives. This is all mirrored in the different criteria for pension benefit withdrawal in different schemes. In 2016 the average normal pension age was equal to 59.4 years for men and 57.5 years for women in the non-OECD economies. With only two economies increasing their retirement ages the long-term age only increase to 60.3 for men and 58.5 for women.

Table 1.5, on the left hand side, shows the rules for normal and early retirement by pension benefit scheme for a person entering the labour force at age 20. In 2016 the average normal pension age across the Asian economies was equal to 59.4 years for men and 57.5 years for women across all schemes and economies. These averages should however be interpreted with caution as they do not say anything about how individuals actually react to these ages in either the schemes or economies. For the OECD as a whole the averages are 64.3 for men and 63.7 for women.

Normal pension age

The lowest normal pension ages equal 50 for women in Sri Lanka and blue collar women in China and 55 for men in Malaysia, Sri Lanka and Thailand. The highest normal pension age is 65 in Hong Kong, China and the Philippines.

In four out of the 11 economies the pension ages still differ between men and women, compared to only two of the OECD countries listed, both of which are equalising the ages.

In three of the 11 economies, different rules apply to different components of the overall retirement-income package and so these are shown separately. In Hong Kong, China and Malaysia the normal retirement age is that for the DC component as it is assumed individuals have a full career. For India it is age 58 as this enables full benefit from all components of the pension system without reduction.

The long-term retirement ages, shown in the right hand columns, indicate that only Indonesia and Singapore are increasing their retirement ages, both reaching age 65. By contrast six of the ten OECD countries listed are increasing their retirement ages. The long-term average for all OECD countries is 65.8 for men and 65.5 for women, both above the highest retirement age for the Asian economies.

Early age

Early pension withdrawal about five years before the normal retirement age is relatively common for the Asian economies.

In most defined benefit and points schemes, the adjustment is simply a parameter of the pension system: the benefit is permanently reduced by x% for each year of early retirement.

In defined contribution systems the size of the annual benefit varies and depends on the age of benefit withdrawals through the accumulated assets and the size of the annuity divisor, though for many Asian economies lump-sum withdrawal is the norm. The annuity divisor is calculated as a function of expected remaining life expectancy and discount rates. In these types of systems there is only an age of early pension withdrawal.

If all of the earliest retirement ages were applied the overall average would be 55.7 for men, compared to 59.4 for the normal retirement age. Similarly the average for women is 54.1 compared to 57.5 for the normal retirement age.

Table 1.5. Early and normal retirement ages for an individual entering the labour market or retiring in 2016 by type of pension scheme

		Individual retiring in 2016			Individual entering the labour market in 2016		
		Scheme	Early age	Normal	Scheme	Early age	Normal
East Asia/Pacific							
China	men	DB/DC	n.a.	60	DB/DC	n.a.	60
	women	DB/DC	n.a.	50/55	DB/DC	n.a.	50/55
Hong Kong, China		DC	60	65	DC	60	65
		T		65	T		65
		Basic		70	Basic		70
Indonesia		DB/DC	flexible	56	DB/DC		65
Malaysia		DC	50	55	DC	50	55
		T	n.a.	60	T	n.a.	60
Philippines		Basic/DB	60	65	Basic/DB	60	65
Singapore		DC	n.a.	64	DC	n.a.	65
Thailand		DB	n.a.	55	DB	n.a.	55
Viet Nam	men	DB	55	60	DB	55	60
	women	DB	50	55	DB	50	55
South Asia							
India		DB	50	58	DB	50	58
		DC		55	DC		55
Pakistan	men	DB	55	60	DB	55	60
	women	DB	50	55	DB	50	55
Sri Lanka	men	DC	n.a.	55	DC	n.a.	55
	women	DC	n.a.	50	DC	n.a.	50
OECD Asia/Pacific							
Australia		T	n.a.	65	T	n.a.	67
		DC	55	..	DC	60	
Canada		Basic/T	n.a.	65	Basic/T	n.a.	65
		DB (ER)	60	65	DB (ER)	60	65
Japan		Basic/DB	60	65	Basic/DB	60	65
Korea		DB	57	61	DB	60	65
New Zealand		Basic	n.a.	65	Basic	n.a.	65
United States		DB	62	66	DB	62	67
		T		65	T	n.a.	65
Other OECD							
France		DB	61.6	61.6	DB	62	63
		Points	56.7	61.6	Points	57	64
Germany		Points	65	65	Points	63	65
Italy	men	NDC	62.8	66.6	NDC	67.4	71.2
	women	NDC	61.8	65.6			
United Kingdom	men	Basic (SP)	n.a.	65	Basic/T	n.a.	68
	women	Basic (SP)	n.a.	63			
		T (PC)	n.a.	63			

Note: The normal retirement age is calculated assuming labour market entry at age 20. DB = defined benefit; DC = defined contribution; n.a. = early retirement or deferral of pension is not available; T = targeted. Where pension ages for men and women differ they are shown as Men/Women.
Source: See Chapter 3 for non-OECD economies and "Country Profiles" available at http://oe.cd/pag for OECD countries.

StatLink http://dx.doi.org/10.1787/888933873212

Chapter 2. Retirement-income indicators

The first two indicators of this chapter are both replacement rates; that is, the ratio of pension benefits to individual earnings. These are given in gross and net terms, taking account of taxes and contributions paid on earnings and on retirement incomes.

The next two indicators are based on pension wealth, again in gross and net terms. Pension wealth, unlike replacement rates, reflects differences in pension ages, indexation of pensions in payment and national life expectancy.

The remainder of Chapter 2 consists of at a glance analyses of pension earnings link, coverage, life expectancy and support ratio, each of which play a key role in pension modelling.

Methodology and assumptions

> The indicators of pension entitlements that follow here in Chapter 2 use the OECD cohort-based pension models. The methodology and assumptions are common to the analysis of all economies, allowing the design of pension systems to be compared directly. This enables the comparison of future entitlements under today's parameters and rules.

The pension entitlements that are presented are those that are currently legislated in the Asian economies. Reforms that have been legislated before publication are included where sufficient information is available. Changes that have already been legislated and are being phased-in gradually and yearly are modelled from the year that they are implemented and onwards.

The values of all pension system parameters reflect the situation in the year 2016 and onwards. The calculations show the pension benefits of a worker who enters the system that year at age 20 and retires after a full career. The main results are shown for a single person. All indexation and valorisation rules follow what is legislated in the baseline scenario.

Career length

The standard OECD definition is used for both the OECD and non-OECD economies. Therefore a full career is defined here as entering the labour market at age 20 and working until standard pension eligibility age, which, of course, varies between economies. The implication is that length of career varies with the statutory retirement age: 35 years for retirement at 55, 40 years for retirement at 60, etc.

Coverage

The pension models presented here include all mandatory pension schemes for private-sector workers, regardless of whether they are public (i.e. they involve payments from government or from social security institutions, as defined in the System of National Accounts) or private. For each economy, the main national scheme for private sector employees is modelled.

Pension entitlements are compared for workers with earnings between 0.5 times and twice the average. This range permits an analysis of future retirement benefits of both the poorest and richest workers.

Economic variables

The comparisons are based on a single set of economic assumptions for all the economies covered. Although the levels of economic growth, wage growth and inflation vary across economies, using a single set of assumptions enables comparison without economic affects. Differences in pension levels therefore reflect differences in actual pension systems and government policies. The baseline assumptions for set out below.

Price inflation is assumed to be 2% per year. **Real earnings** are assumed to grow by 1.25% per year on average (given the assumption for price inflation, this implies nominal wage growth of 3.275%). **Individual earnings** are assumed to grow in line with the economy-wide average. This means that the individual is assumed to remain at the same point in the earnings distribution, earning the same percentage of average earnings in every year of the working life. The **real rate of return** on funded, defined-contribution pensions is assumed to be 3% per year. Administrative charges, fee structures and the cost of buying an annuity are assumed to result in a defined contribution conversion factor of 90% applied to the accumulated defined contribution wealth when calculating the annuity. The **real discount rate** (for actuarial calculations) is assumed to be 2% per year.

The baseline modelling uses economy-specific projections of mortality rate from the United Nations population database for every year from 2016 to 2080.

The calculations assume that benefits from defined contribution plans are paid in the form of a price-indexed life annuity at an actuarially fair price assuming perfect foresight. This is calculated from the mortality projections once the conversion factor is taken into account. If people withdraw the money in alternative ways, the capital sum at the time of retirement is the same: it is only the way that the benefits are spread that is changed. Similarly, the notional annuity rate in notional accounts schemes is (in most cases) calculated from mortality data using the indexation rules and discounting assumptions employed by the respective economy.

Taxes and social security contributions

The modelling assumes that tax systems and social security contributions remain unchanged in the future. This implicitly means that "value" parameters, such as tax allowances or contribution ceilings, are adjusted annually in line with average earnings, while "rate" parameters, such as the personal income tax schedule and social security contribution rates, remain unchanged.

Gross replacement rates

> Gross replacement rates, showing pension benefit as a share of individual lifetime average earnings, vary greatly across Asia, from 37.5% in Thailand to 87.4% in India. These are the extremes for average earners but estimates are also given at 50% and 200% of average earnings. Replacement rates generally decline as earnings increase and are usually higher for men than for women.

Often, the replacement rate is expressed as the ratio of the pension over the final earnings before retirement. However, the indicator used here shows the pension benefit as a share of individual lifetime average earnings (re-valued in line with economy-wide earnings growth). Under the baseline assumptions, workers earn the same percentage of economy-wide average earnings throughout their career. In this case, lifetime average re-valued earnings and individual final earnings are identical.

For workers at average earnings, the average for the OECD countries of the gross replacement rate from mandatory pensions is 52.9% for men and 52.3% for women. There is little variation across Asia/Pacific OECD economies, with Canada at the top of the range, offering replacement rates of 41.0% and Australia at the bottom with only 32.2%. The rates for the non-OECD economies do have a wide range, going from 87% for India to 38% for Thailand, followed by Sri Lanka and Hong Kong, China at just over 40%. Regional variation also exists with both India and Pakistan having a replacement rate approximately double that of Sri Lanka, whilst the majority of the remaining Asia/Pacific economies have replacement rates between 60% and 75%. The non-Asian OECD economies tend to have lower replacement rates with Italy and, to a lesser degree, France being among the exceptions with replacement rates of 83% and 61% respectively.

Low earners – workers earning only half the mean – have higher replacement rates than mean earners: on average, 65% for the OECD. This reflects the fact that most economies attempt to protect low income workers from old-age poverty. The cross-economy variation of replacement rates at this earnings level is much higher than it is for pensions of those who earn twice the average. The highest gross replacement rates for low earners are found in China at 96%, which means that full-career workers with permanently low earnings have approximately the same income, upon retirement, as when they were working. The lowest rate is observed in Thailand, which has a replacement rate of 39% for low earners. Australia has the highest replacement rate amongst Asian OECD economies at 83%, more than twice that of Germany.

For high earners – working earning twice the mean – India again offers the highest pensions, with a replacement rate of 86%, followed by Viet Nam which has a steady replacement rate of 75% across all the earnings levels. The variation across economies in replacement rates for high earners is much smaller than it is for people on low or average pay. Thailand is again at the bottom of the rankings for the non-OECD economies, at 19%, though it is higher than the United Kingdom. Again the majority of the non-OECD economies have higher replacement rates than their OECD counterparts, with the exception of Italy. Seven of the eleven non-OECD economies have a higher replacement rate than the OECD average of 44.5%, compared to only two of the ten OECD countries listed. The replacement rates in Australia and Canada are under half the level for low earners. For Korea the replacement rates are at about one-third of the level for low earners, while for New Zealand and the United Kingdom they are only at one-quarter of the level.

For women the replacement rates are at best equal, but are generally below, those for men, without exception. Whilst most OECD countries have the same replacement rates for men and women it is noticeable that all the non-OECD economies, apart from the Philippines, Thailand and Viet Nam, have lower replacement rates for women than for men.

Table 2.1. Gross pension replacement rates by earnings, men and women

	Men			Women				Men			Women		
Individual earnings (% average)	50	100	200	50	100	200	Individual earnings (% average)	50	100	200	50	100	200
East Asia/Pacific							**OECD Asia/Pacific**						
China	96.0	76.0	66.0	82.6	65.1	56.3	Australia	82.8	32.2	32.1	80.0	29.4	29.3
Hong Kong, China	53.8	42.2	37.0	51.1	38.2	32.3	Canada	54.1	41.0	21.4	54.1	41.0	21.4
Indonesia	62.1	62.1	61.0	57.8	57.8	56.7	Japan	47.8	34.6	26.2	47.8	34.6	26.2
Malaysia	70.3	69.4	68.4	64.9	64.1	63.1	Korea	58.5	39.3	21.5	58.5	39.3	21.5
Philippines	73.8	71.9	70.1	73.8	71.9	70.1	New Zealand	80.0	40.0	20.0	80.0	40.0	20.0
Singapore	53.1	53.1	31.5	47.3	47.3	28.0	United States	48.3	38.3	27.1	48.3	38.3	27.1
Thailand	38.8	37.5	18.8	38.8	37.5	18.8	**Other OECD**						
Viet Nam	75.0	75.0	75.0	75.0	75.0	75.0	France	60.5	60.5	51.8	60.5	60.5	51.8
							Germany	38.2	38.2	29.7	38.2	38.2	29.7
South Asia							Italy	83.1	83.1	83.1	83.1	83.1	83.1
India	87.4	87.4	85.9	83.1	83.1	81.5	United Kingdom	44.3	22.1	11.1	44.3	22.1	11.1
Pakistan	80.0	80.0	44.9	78.6	70.0	39.3	**OECD**	**64.9**	**52.9**	**44.5**	**64.4**	**52.3**	**44.1**
Sri Lanka	40.6	40.6	40.6	33.9	33.9	33.9							

Source: OECD pension models.

StatLink http://dx.doi.org/10.1787/888933873231

Figure 2.1. Gross pension replacement rates by earnings, low and average earners

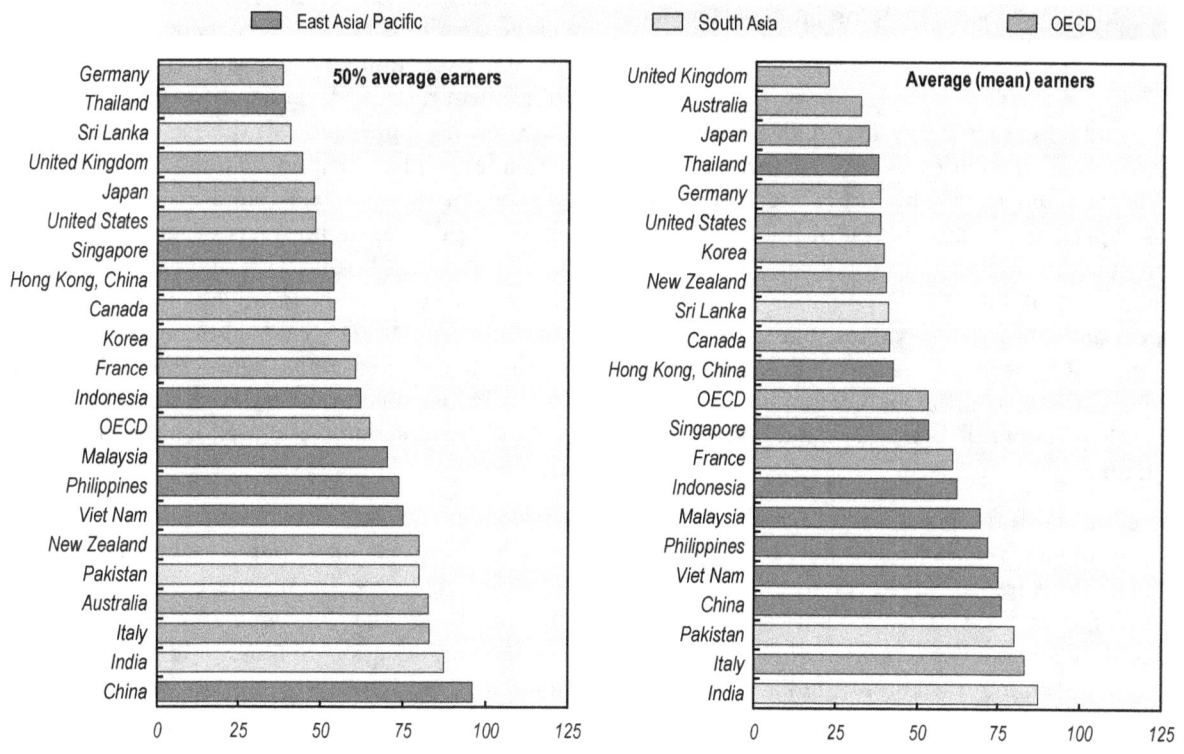

Source: OECD pension models

StatLink http://dx.doi.org/10.1787/888933873250

Net replacement rates

> Net replacement rates show greater diversity than the gross replacement rates. They range from 39.3% in Thailand to 99.3% in India. These are the extremes for average earners but findings are also given at 50% and 200% of average earnings. Replacement rates generally decline as earnings increase, though Malaysia, Viet Nam and Italy do not follow this premise, and are usually higher for men than for women. Results for China and India are the highest especially for low and average earners. As with gross replacement rates Thailand is at the bottom of the rankings.

The net replacement rate is defined as the individual net pension entitlement divided by net pre-retirement earnings, taking account of personal income taxes and social security contributions paid by workers and pensioners. The personal tax system plays an important role in old-age support. Pensioners often do not pay social security contributions and, as personal income taxes are progressive and pension entitlements are usually lower than earnings before retirement, the average tax rate on pension income is typically less than the tax rate on earned income. In addition, most income tax systems give preferential treatment either to pension incomes or to pensioners, by giving additional allowances or credits to older people. Therefore, net replacement rates are usually higher than gross replacement rates.

For average earners, the net replacement rate across OECD countries is 63.1% for men and 62.5% for women, which is 10% higher than for gross replacement rates. Seven of the non-OECD economies are higher than this average for men, whereas out of the OECD countries listed, only France and Italy have values higher than the average. Replacement rates within Asia are similar across the different geographical regions and also between OECD and non-OECD economies.

Low earners – workers earning only half the mean – have higher replacement rates than average earners: on average, 73.9% for the OECD. This reflects the fact that most countries attempt to protect low income workers from old-age poverty. The cross-economy variation of replacement rates at this earnings level is much lower within the OECD than for the Asian economies. The highest net replacement rate for low earners is found in China at 104.4%, which means that full-career workers with permanently low earnings have more money when they retire than when they were working. Australia and India also have replacement rates at this earnings level that are just below full replacement, at 95.0% and 99.3% respectively. The lowest rates are observed in Thailand where full-career workers on half average earnings have only a 40.3% replacement rate. The replacement rates in Indonesia, Malaysia, Singapore and Thailand are lower at this earnings level when compared to average earners.

For high earners – workers earning twice the mean – the OECD average drops to 55.0%, with all OECD countries having lower replacement rates at this earnings level than at average or 50% average earnings. For Asia the same trend applies with the exception of Malaysia, and in fact the replacement rate in Malaysia at this earnings level is the second highest for all the East Asia/Pacific economies, just behind India. The lowest replacement rate is again found in Thailand. The gap to the other economies has widened compared to other earnings levels, with India, Malaysia, the Philippines and Viet Nam all having a rate over four times that of Thailand. On comparison with the 50% average earnings figure, the replacement rate for Pakistan is just over half at 45.4% and that for New Zealand and the United Kingdom are less than one-third of their earlier levels.

For women the net replacement rates are at best equal to those for men, but are generally lower, and this is the case for all the economies listed. The rates in the Philippines, Thailand and Viet Nam are identical to those of men, whereas in China and Sri Lanka the replacement rates for women are around 85% those for men across all the earnings levels. This lower level is mainly due to the lower retirement age for women than men, meaning fewer years of contribution.

2. RETIREMENT-INCOME INDICATORS

Table 2.2. Net pension replacement rates by earnings, men and women

Individual earnings (% average)	Men			Women			Individual earnings (% average)	Men			Women		
	50	100	200	50	100	200		50	100	200	50	100	200
East Asia/Pacific							**OECD Asia/Pacific**						
China	104.4	83.2	74.9	89.7	71.5	64.6	Australia	95.0	42.6	47.0	91.8	38.8	42.9
Hong Kong, China	56.7	44.5	41.4	53.8	40.4	36.1	Canada	62.2	53.4	30.2	62.2	53.4	30.2
Indonesia	65.3	66.0	64.5	60.8	61.6	60.0	Japan	52.6	40.0	31.0	52.6	40.0	31.0
Malaysia	81.4	85.5	91.3	75.1	78.9	84.3	Korea	63.8	45.1	26.3	63.8	45.1	26.3
Philippines	86.8	88.1	90.6	86.8	88.1	90.6	New Zealand	80.7	43.2	23.7	80.7	43.2	23.7
Singapore	57.4	58.6	34.9	51.1	52.2	31.1	United States	59.9	49.1	37.1	59.9	49.1	37.1
Thailand	40.3	39.3	19.3	40.3	39.3	19.3							
Viet Nam	81.5	81.5	81.5	81.5	81.5	81.5	**Other OECD**						
							France	70.4	74.5	65.8	70.4	74.5	65.8
South Asia							Germany	54.7	50.5	38.9	54.7	50.5	38.9
India	99.3	99.3	97.6	94.4	94.4	92.6	Italy	93.0	93.2	91.4	93.0	93.2	91.4
Pakistan	80.8	80.8	45.4	79.4	70.7	39.7	United Kingdom	52.1	29.0	16.3	52.1	29.0	16.3
Sri Lanka	44.2	44.2	44.4	36.9	36.9	37.1	**OECD**	**73.9**	**63.1**	**55.0**	**73.4**	**62.5**	**54.4**

Source: OECD pension models.

StatLink http://dx.doi.org/10.1787/888933873269

Figure 2.2. Net pension replacement rates by earnings, low and average earners

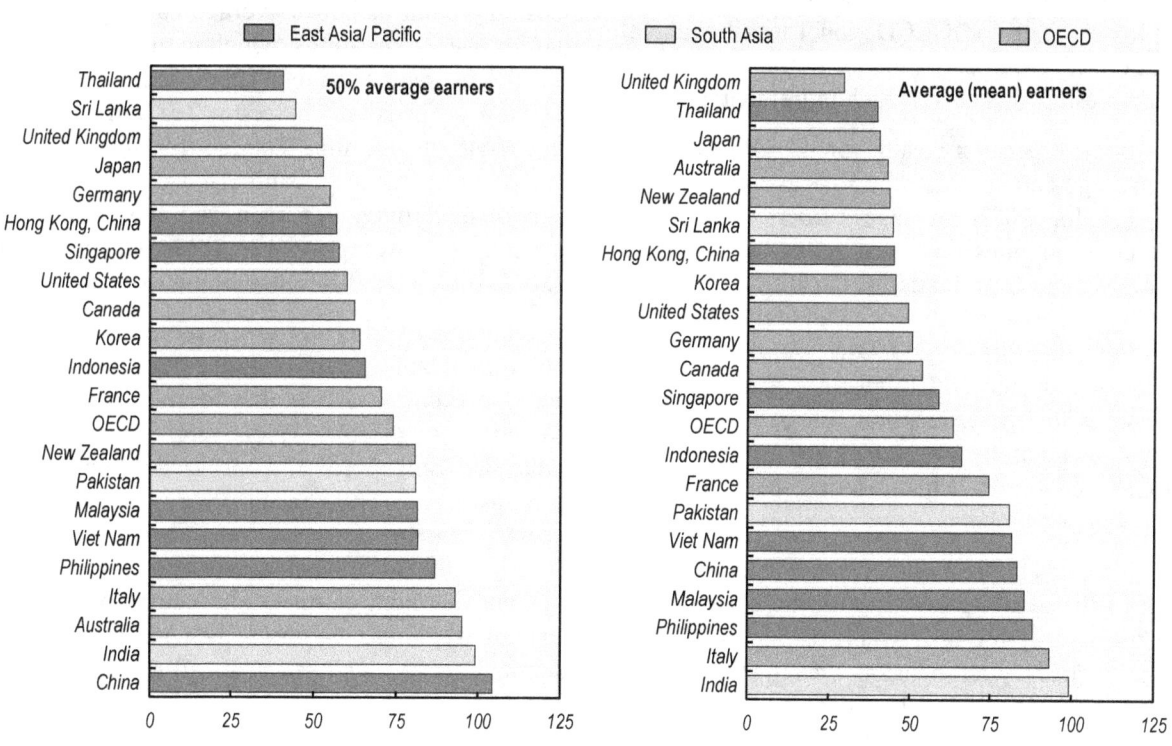

Source: OECD pension models.

StatLink http://dx.doi.org/10.1787/888933873288

Gross pension wealth

> Gross pension wealth, indicating the magnitude of the total pension promise, ranges, for men, from a high of 20.4 years of earnings in China for low earners to a low of 4 in Thailand for high earners. The value for women in China is actually even higher at 21.0, meaning that someone on 50% average earnings throughout the lifetime has a mandatory pension worth 21.0 times their earnings level at retirement, though the values in Viet Nam are even higher for women at 22.8 across all earnings levels.

Pension wealth shows the size of the lump sum that would be needed to buy a flow of pension payments equivalent to that promised by the mandatory pension system in each economy. Pension wealth is measured and expressed as a multiple of gross annual individual earnings. It is shown here for workers with earnings of 50%, 100% and 200% of the average, separately for men and women. For a fuller picture though consideration needs to be given to both retirement ages and life expectancy variation across economies. For example, the general retirement age within OECD countries is 65 or 67, whereas for the non-OECD economies it is generally either 55 or 60 for men. Whilst it is shown later that the life expectancy levels in non-OECD economies are lower than for OECD countries the actual duration of retirement is longer in the non-OECD economies for those who reach retirement age.

The average pension wealth for the OECD is 9.7 for average earners, 12.0 for 50% average earners and 8.1 for 200% average earners. The other OECD economies are generally below these averages apart from France at the 100% and 200% earnings levels and Italy across all earnings levels. For the Asian/Pacific OECD economies they are all lower than the OECD average at all earnings levels, with the exception of Australia and New Zealand at the low earners level. For the non-OECD economies China, India, Malaysia and Viet Nam are higher at all earnings levels.

Viet Nam has the highest pension wealth of all for each of the earnings levels, with the exception of the 50% level for men where China is slightly higher. The lowest pension wealth figures are found in Indonesia for low earners, at 7.8. The value for China is nearly three times that of Thailand for men with lifetime earnings equivalent to 50% average within their economy.

The level of pension wealth either remains steady or declines as the level of earnings increases in all the other economies. In Thailand for 200% average earners the level of pension wealth is approximately half that for 50% average earners. Likewise in Japan, Singapore and the United States, the levels are around 60%, though in all cases the actual lump-sum value for 200% average earners is at least double. For example the lump sum in Thailand for 50% average earners is $8.4 * 0.5 = 4.2$ times average earnings, compared to $4.1 * 2.0 = 8.2$ times average earnings for those at the 200% earnings level. For New Zealand the pension wealth at 200% average earnings is half that for average earnings, which in turn is half that for 50% average earnings. This is expected as the mandatory pension in New Zealand is not dependent on earnings and so for all earnings levels the pension wealth is worth 8.9 times individual earnings for men and 9.5 individual earnings for women. The difference between sexes is due to the difference in life expectancies.

As mentioned earlier the levels of pension wealth for women are generally higher than those for men. No economy has higher levels for men than women, though the levels are identical for Malaysia, Singapore and Sri Lanka across all earnings levels. The variation for women is also greater than that for men, ranging from 22.8 in Viet Nam for 50% average earnings to 4.5 in the Thailand for high earners. The rate of decline in pension wealth as earnings increase is virtually identical between the sexes for all the economies included.

Table 2.3. Gross pension wealth by earnings, men and women

	Men			Women				Men			Women		
Individual earnings (% average)	50	100	200	50	100	200	Individual earnings (% average)	50	100	200	50	100	200
East Asia/Pacific							**OECD Asia/Pacific**						
China	20.4	16.1	14.0	21.0	16.5	14.3	Australia	15.0	5.8	5.8	15.9	5.8	5.8
Hong Kong, China	10.4	8.2	7.2	11.9	8.9	7.5	Canada	10.4	7.9	4.1	11.2	8.5	4.4
Indonesia	7.8	7.8	7.7	8.6	8.6	8.5	Japan	9.1	6.6	5.0	10.9	7.9	6.0
Malaysia	16.3	16.1	15.9	16.3	16.1	15.9	Korea	11.0	7.4	4.0	13.2	8.8	4.8
Philippines	9.3	9.1	8.8	11.4	11.1	10.8	New Zealand	17.8	8.9	4.4	19.0	9.5	4.7
Singapore	10.4	10.4	6.1	10.4	10.4	6.1	United States	8.4	6.7	4.7	8.9	7.0	5.0
Thailand	8.4	8.1	4.1	9.2	8.9	4.5	**Other OECD**						
Viet Nam	17.1	17.1	17.1	22.8	22.8	22.8	France	11.8	11.8	10.1	13.5	13.5	11.6
							Germany	8.3	8.3	6.4	9.0	9.0	7.0
South Asia							Italy	13.3	13.3	13.3	15.0	15.0	15.0
India	15.2	15.2	15.0	16.1	16.1	15.9	United Kingdom	8.9	4.4	2.2	9.5	4.8	2.4
Pakistan	11.8	11.8	6.6	14.7	13.1	7.3	**OECD**	**12.0**	**9.7**	**8.1**	**13.3**	**10.7**	**9.0**
Sri Lanka	8.7	8.7	8.7	8.7	8.7	8.7							

Source: OECD pension models.

StatLink http://dx.doi.org/10.1787/888933873307

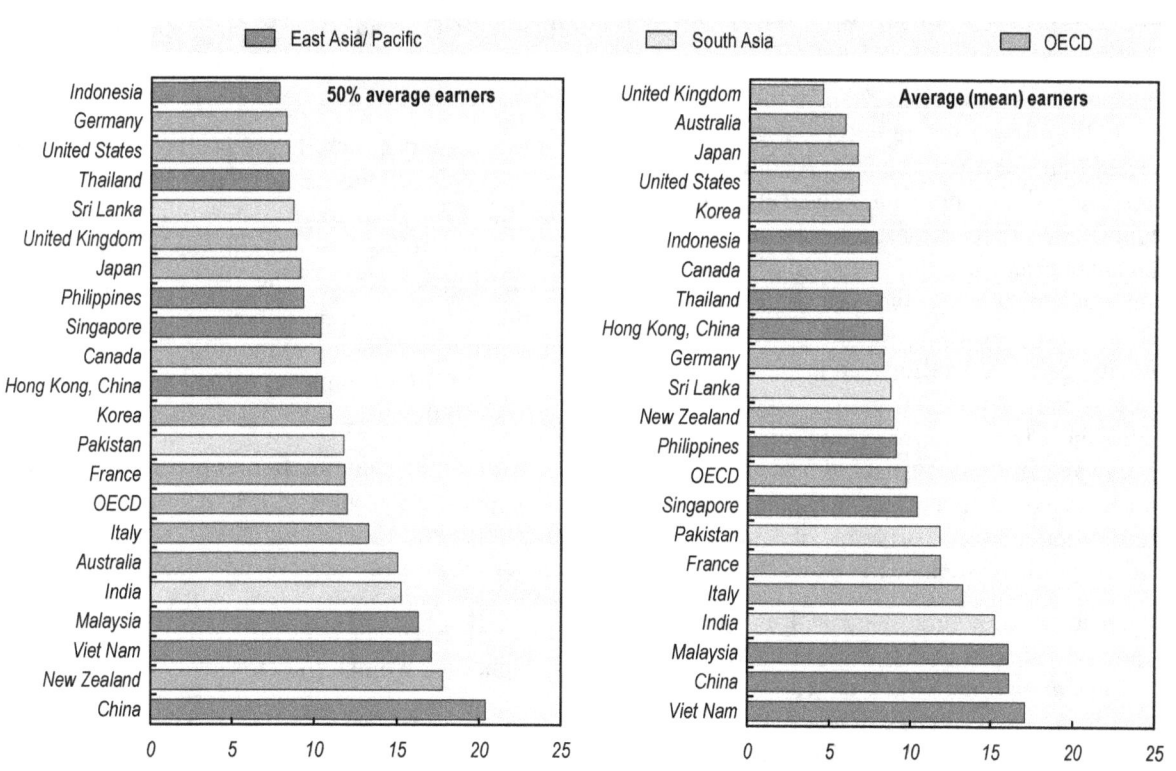

Figure 2.3. Gross pension wealth by earnings, low and average earners

Source: OECD pension models.

StatLink http://dx.doi.org/10.1787/888933873326

Net pension wealth

> Net pension wealth, the present value of the flow of pension benefits, again varies by economy, ranging from 22.1 for men in China (24.8 for women in Viet Nam) for low earners to 4.2 and 4.6 for men and women in Thailand at high earnings level. Malaysia and Viet Nam have the highest levels for both average and high earners.

Replacement rates give an indication of the pension promise relative to individual earnings, but they are not comprehensive measures of cumulated pension payments; they look only at the benefit level relative to individual earnings at the point of retirement, or more generally at a given, later age. For a full picture, life expectancy, normal retirement age and indexation of pension benefits must also be taken into account. Together, these determine for how long the pension benefit is paid, and how its value evolves over time. Net pension wealth – a measure of the stock of future discounted flows of pension benefits after taxes and social contributions – takes account of these factors. It can be thought of as the total net benefits that will be received on average from the mandatory retirement-income schemes.

In defined benefit systems there is often no or a weak link between the replacement rate and the expected duration of benefit withdrawal. Of course, in the long run, ensuring financial sustainability imposes a trade-off between the replacement rate and the duration of retirement. When retirement ages and pension benefits are held constant, pension wealth increases with longevity gains. In defined contribution systems there is a more direct link between the size of the benefit and the expected duration of benefit withdrawals. In these systems the pension wealth measure is equal to the accumulated assets and therefore independent of longevity increases as these automatically reduce the benefits.

Net pension wealth at individual earnings equal to average worker earnings is highest in Malaysia at 19.8 times annual individual net earnings for men and women, but the highest level for women is found in Viet Nam at 24.8. The lowest pension wealth is found in Indonesia at 8.3 times for men and 9.2 for women, due to lower replacement rates.

The average for the OECD countries is 13.6 for low earners, 11.6 for average earners and 10.0 for high earners. All of the OECD countries have decreasing pension wealth levels as earnings increase. As with the gross pension wealth the values for New Zealand roughly half on each doubling of earnings as the mandatory pension is not affected by earnings but rather residency rules.

For high earners the non-OECD Asian economies dominate with China, India, Malaysia, the Philippines and Viet Nam having values above the OECD average, with none of the Asian OECD countries having a higher value than the OECD average. The values in both Malaysia and Viet Nam are approximately twice that of the OECD average. Even the variation within the other OECD countries is apparent with Italy having a net pension wealth over four times that of the United Kingdom for high earners.

For low earners China, India, Malaysia, Singapore and Viet Nam all have a net pension wealth higher than the OECD average. The value in China at 22.1 is over twice the value in Indonesia. For the OECD only four of the economies, namely Australia, France, Italy and New Zealand have a net pension wealth above the OECD average. The remaining OECD countries all have similar values between 10.0 and 12.0.

For women the same pattern is repeated as for the gross pension wealth, in that only Malaysia, Singapore and Sri Lanka having the same net pension wealth figures for men than women. The remaining economies, both OECD and non-OECD all have net pension wealth estimates that are higher for women than for men.

2. RETIREMENT-INCOME INDICATORS | 29

Table 2.4. Net pension wealth by earnings, men and women

	Men			Women				Men			Women		
Individual earnings (% average)	50	100	200	50	100	200	Individual earnings (% average)	50	100	200	50	100	200
East Asia/Pacific							**OECD Asia/Pacific**						
China	22.1	17.7	15.9	22.8	18.2	16.4	Australia	17.2	7.7	8.5	18.3	7.7	8.5
Hong Kong, China	11.0	8.6	8.0	12.6	9.4	8.4	Canada	11.9	10.2	5.8	12.8	11.0	6.2
Indonesia	8.2	8.3	8.1	9.1	9.2	9.0	Japan	10.0	7.6	5.9	12.0	9.2	7.1
Malaysia	18.9	19.8	21.2	18.9	19.8	21.2	Korea	12.0	8.5	4.9	14.3	10.1	5.9
Philippines	10.9	11.1	11.4	13.4	13.6	14.0	New Zealand	17.9	9.6	5.3	19.1	10.2	5.6
Singapore	11.2	11.4	6.8	11.2	11.4	6.8	United States	10.5	8.6	6.5	11.0	9.0	6.8
Thailand	8.7	8.5	4.2	9.6	9.3	4.6							
Viet Nam	18.6	18.6	18.6	24.8	24.8	24.8	**Other OECD**						
							France	13.7	14.5	12.8	15.7	16.6	14.7
South Asia							Germany	11.8	10.9	8.4	12.9	12.0	9.2
India	17.3	17.3	17.0	18.3	18.3	18.0	Italy	14.8	14.9	14.6	16.8	16.8	16.5
Pakistan	11.9	11.9	6.7	14.8	13.2	7.4	United Kingdom	10.5	5.8	3.3	11.2	6.2	3.5
Sri Lanka	9.5	9.5	9.5	9.5	9.5	9.5	**OECD**	**13.6**	**11.6**	**10.0**	**15.2**	**12.8**	**11.1**

Source: OECD pension models.

StatLink http://dx.doi.org/10.1787/888933873345

Figure 2.4. Net pension wealth by earnings, low and average earners

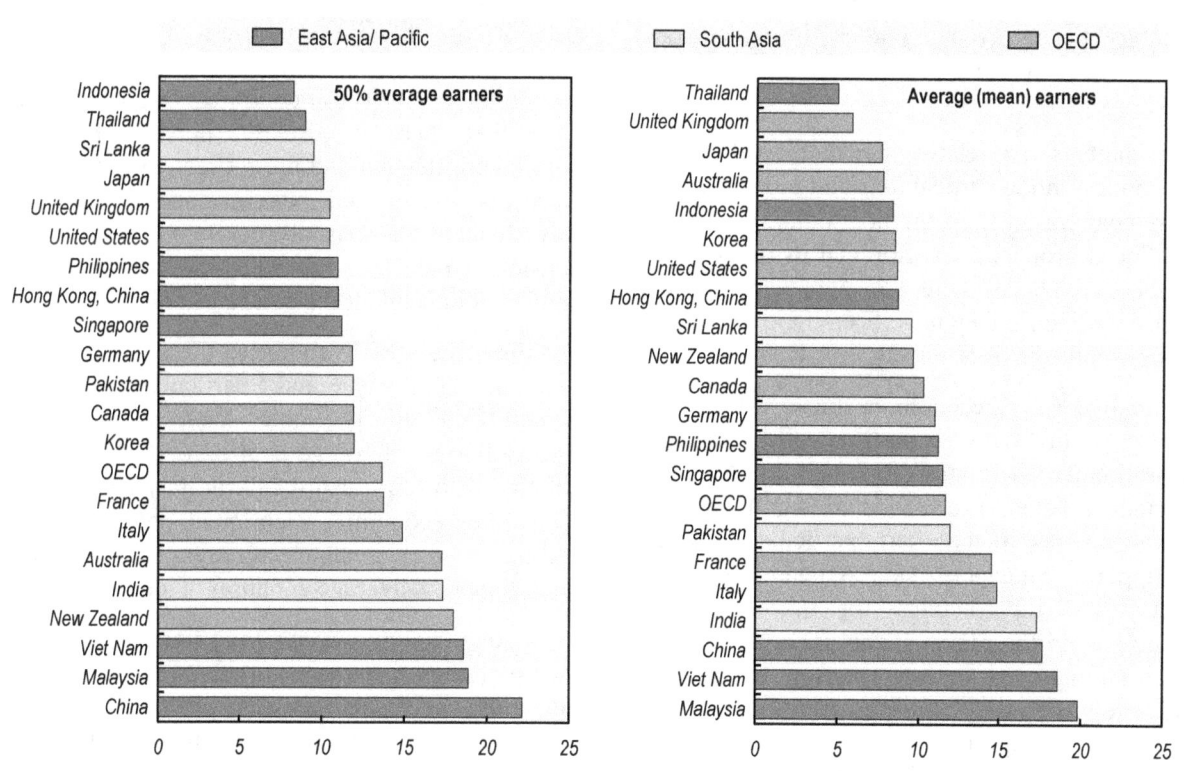

Source: OECD pension models.

StatLink http://dx.doi.org/10.1787/888933873364

PENSIONS AT A GLANCE ASIA/PACIFIC 2018 © OECD 2018

Pension earnings link

> The pension earnings link, showing the link between pension entitlements and individual earnings, varies widely between economies. Levels in Indonesia, Hong Kong, China and particularly New Zealand show that there is virtually no link, whereas Viet Nam, China and Pakistan display a strong link between pension entitlements and individual earnings. The relative pension levels are used here to illustrate the link between individual pre-retirement earnings and pension benefits in each economy. They are shown for individual earnings from 0.5 to 2 times average earnings levels.

The strength of the link between pension entitlements and individual earnings is measured using the relative pension level, that is, the gross individual pension divided by average earnings (rather than by average earnings as in the replacement rate results). It is best seen as an indicator of pension adequacy, since it shows the benefit level that a pensioner will receive in relation to average earnings in the respective economy. Individual replacement rates may be quite high, but the pensioner may still receive only a small fraction of economy-wide average earnings. If, for example, a low-income worker has a replacement rate of 100%, the benefit will only amount to 50% of economy-wide average earnings. For an average earner, the replacement rate and the relative pension level will be the same.

The charts show relative pension levels in the economies on the vertical axis and individual pre-retirement earnings on the horizontal. Economies have been grouped by region and by membership of the OECD. As there are eight economies in East Asia/Pacific they have been divided into two groups on the basis of results.

In the first set of economies (Panel A), there is little or no link between pension entitlements and pre-retirement earnings for any of the four economies listed. The ranges are small for all of the economies in the chart, particularly for the Philippines, Singapore and Thailand. This is in contrast to the findings for the other four economies in the region (Panel B) which show a much stronger link between pension entitlements and pre-retirement earnings. In Viet Nam for example the range is 37% to 150% compared to only 19% to 37% for Thailand. For Viet Nam there is also no ceiling to pensionable earnings as it is paid in a lump sum which has been converted to an annual entitlement. Thailand has a different system in that the maximum contribution level applies for earnings not much below the average, which explains why the graph levels at just under 100% of average earnings.

Panel C covers the economies in South Asia, all of which indicate a link between pension entitlements and pre-retirement earnings, but to different degrees. In both India and Sri Lanka there is a clearly linear relationship between earnings and pension entitlement, whereas the ceiling in Pakistan levels the values at just over average earnings.

The remaining two charts, Panel D and Panel E, are for the OECD countries, with the first covering the Asia/Pacific economies and the second the other OECD countries. In Panel D it is clear that there is virtually no link between pension entitlement and pre-retirement earnings in Australia, Japan and New Zealand. In fact in New Zealand there is absolutely no link as the pension is paid at a flat rate based on residency and is not dependent on earnings at all.

For the other OECD countries there is very little link in Germany, and particularly in the United Kingdom. In France there is a slightly greater link as the range is 30% to 104%, but the country with the greatest link is Italy (In Italy as with other economies mentioned previously the ceiling on pensionable earnings is set above three times the average economy-wide earnings).

With some economies applying limits to pension incomes, and others to the levels of contributions, the link between pension entitlements and individual earnings will be broken at some earnings level, even though it evidently existed prior this level.

2. RETIREMENT-INCOME INDICATORS | 31

Figure 2.5. The link between pre-retirement earnings and pension entitlements

Gross pension entitlement as a proportion of economy-wide average earnings

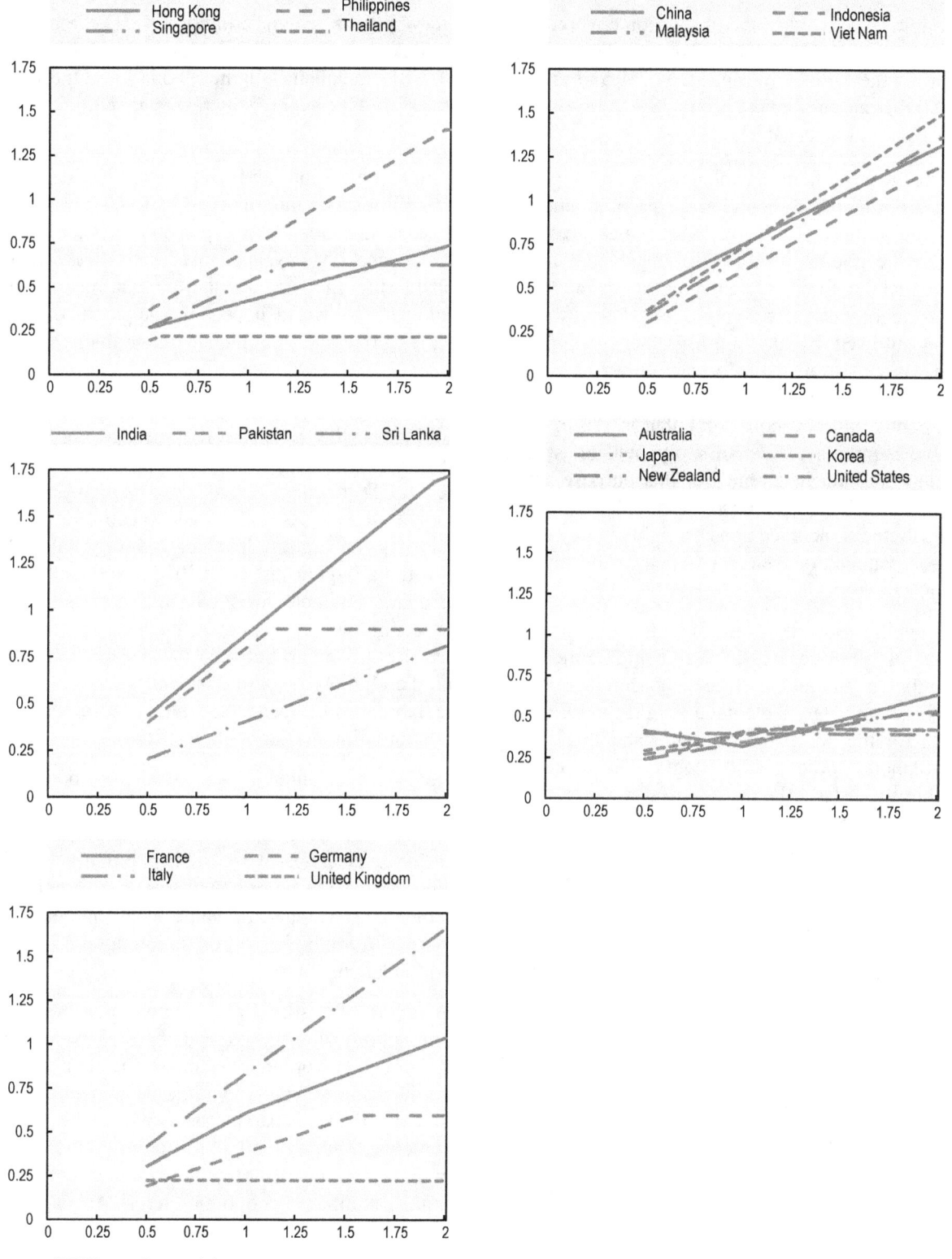

Source: OECD pension models.

StatLink http://dx.doi.org/10.1787/888933873383

Coverage

> The level of coverage, the proportion covered by mandatory pension schemes, in non-OECD economies ranges from 55.4% in Hong Kong, China to only 3.1% in Pakistan, for the population aged 15 to 64. In contrast the OECD average is 64.7% and is as high as 75.0% in Japan. For the labour force the non-OECD economies range from 78.9% to 10.3%, whilst the OECD average increases to 85.6%, with Japan again highest at 95.4%.

Coverage is defined as the proportion of people that are covered by mandatory pension schemes. For the purposes of this report the measures used are i) the population aged 15 to 64, and ii) the active labour force. The coverage percentage is a measure of how effectively a pension system is being utilised by the pre-retirement population and can act as an indicator of future trends. The coverage value is expressed as the percentage of the population or labour force that is classified as active members of a mandatory pension system during the indicated year. For this purpose active members include those that have either contributed or accrued pension rights in any of the major mandatory pension schemes during the indicated year.

For OECD countries as a whole there is very little variation between countries using either the population or labour force measurement. The average coverage percentage within the OECD is 65% for the population measure and 86% using the labour force methodology. The exception within the listed OECD countries is Korea which has noticeably lower values compared to the OECD average, though it is still considerably higher than most of the other economies within the region, with the exception of Hong Kong, China and Singapore.

The remaining Asian, non-OECD, economies vary considerably in the levels of coverage using either measurement. Of these economies only Sri Lanka of the South Asian economies has more than 14% of the population aged 15 to 64 covered by a mandatory pension scheme, whereas its neighbours, India and Pakistan, have less than 7% covered by a scheme. The picture improves slightly for the East Asia/Pacific economies with Hong Kong, China and Singapore having over 44% of their populations aged 15 to 64 covered by at least one mandatory pension scheme, with China and Malaysia close to 30%. When considering the size of the populations in this region of the world it becomes apparent that the lack of coverage is a global rather than regional issue.

The level of coverage does improve in Asia when looking at the labour force measure but non-OECD increases are generally less than those of the OECD countries listed, despite them starting from a higher base. Sri Lanka again for South Asia has the highest level of coverage, at 24%, with India having just over 10% coverage and no do being available for Pakistan. The position of the economies is generally unchanged between measures. The gap between the Asian economies and the OECD as a whole widens when looking at the labour force measure, 61.1%, as opposed to the population measure, 46.7%.

The average figures for Asia for both the population aged 15 to 64 and the labour force are heavily influenced by the low percentage values for India. Because of the high population within India if it was to be removed from the calculation of the Asia average, the value would increase by nearly 6% for both the population aged 15 to 64 and the labour force.

Coverage statistics are better analysed in conjunction with life expectancy and population projections, in order to estimate the numbers of people actually involved rather than percentage. Analysis of these characteristics will highlight the problems that may arise if nothing is done to combat the poor levels of coverage that exist within a number of economies across Asia.

2. RETIREMENT-INCOME INDICATORS | 33

Table 2.5. Membership of mandatory pension schemes by population and labour force

Economy	Year	Members	Percentage of population aged 15 to 65	Percentage of labour force	Economy	Year	Members	Percentage of population aged 15 to 65	Percentage of labour force
East Asia/Pacific					**OECD Asia/Pacific**				
China	2017	403 000 000	39.7%	51.2%	Australia	2005	9 578 000	69.7%	90.7%
Hong Kong, China	2018	2 792 000	52.4%	70.7%	Canada	2009	16 417 000	70.0%	87.4%
Indonesia	2016	22 633 082	13.1%	17.8%	Japan	2005	63 560 000	75.0%	95.4%
Malaysia	2017	7 110 517	33.5%	46.0%	Korea	2011	19 885 900	54.2%	79.9%
Philippines	2014	12 193 170	19.0%	27.3%	New Zealand				
Singapore	2018	2 000 000	49.6%	61.2%	United States	2005	141 129 000	71.4%	92.2%
Thailand	2016	14 041 681	28.6%	35.9%					
Viet Nam	2015	12 574 509	19.2%	21.9%	**Other G7**				
					France	2005	24 319 400	61.4%	87.3%
South Asia					Germany	2005	36 156 000	65.6%	86.9%
India	2018	47 092 872	5.5%	9.1%	Italy	2005	22 146 000	57.1%	90.1%
Pakistan	2018	7 203 344	6.3%	10.3%	United Kingdom	2005	28 402 200	71.5%	93.2%
Sri Lanka	2015	2 600 000	19.0%	29.8%	OECD			64.7%	85.7%

Source: World Bank Pension Database; National reports.

StatLink http://dx.doi.org/10.1787/888933873402

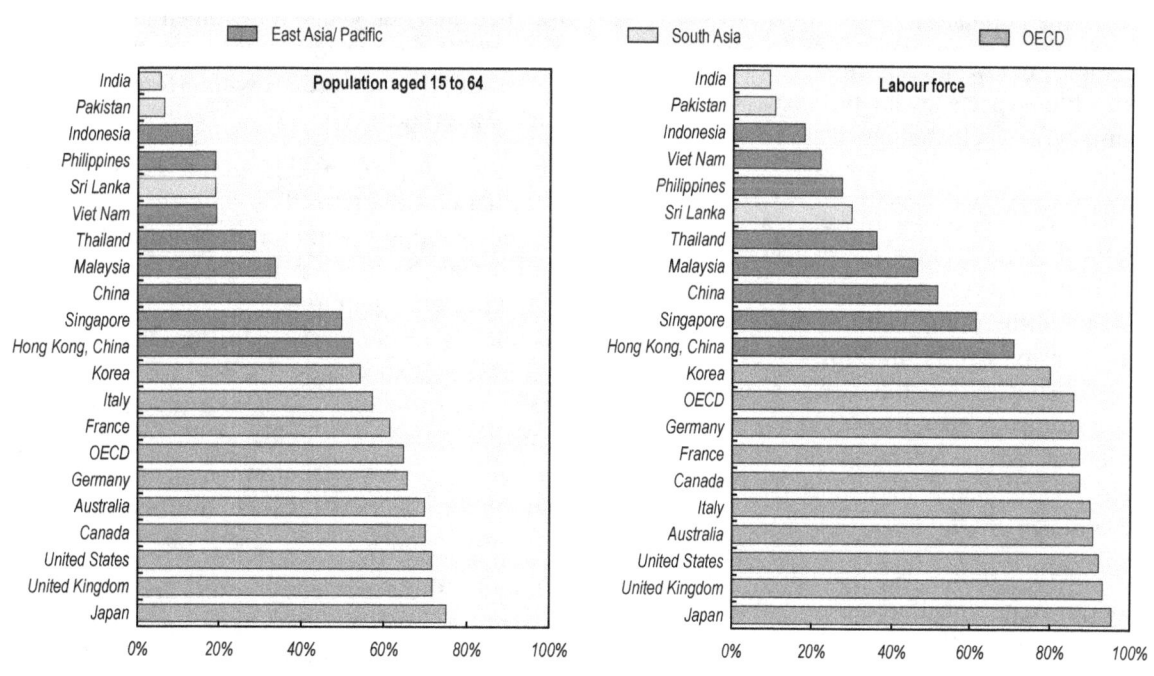

Figure 2.6. Coverage of mandatory pension schemes by population and labour force

Source: World Bank Pension Database; National reports.

StatLink http://dx.doi.org/10.1787/888933873421

PENSIONS AT A GLANCE ASIA/PACIFIC 2018 © OECD 2018

Life expectancy

> Life expectancy at birth in virtually all non-OECD Asian economies is lower than for all the OECD countries covered. The exceptions are Hong Kong, China and Singapore which have life expectancies higher than Australia, Canada, Germany, New Zealand, the United Kingdom and the United States. In fact only Japan has a higher life expectancy than Hong Kong, China. Life expectancy for women in Pakistan is nearly 20 years less than in Japan but if survival to 65 is assumed then the difference drops to exactly 10 years, which will impact greatly on future pension systems.

Information on life expectancy predictions is essential to pension modelling as a guide to the duration that pensions will be claimed. Recently, in many OECD countries life expectancy data has been used to determine future retirement ages and its consideration in any analysis is worthwhile.

Information is available at 2015-20 and is calculated at two different points in time, namely, at birth and age 65. The latter is obviously conditional upon surviving to age 65 but gives a greater indication of the duration of pension receipt. In addition to this life expectancy estimates for 2060-65 are also provided, again dependent on survival to age 65 initially. These are particularly relevant when considering the ageing of the population.

The graphs below for all three indicators show that the life expectancy in the non-OECD Asian economies is well below that of the OECD countries.

The first graph covering life expectancy at birth indicates that the average life expectancy for men and is below 70 years of age in India, Indonesia, Pakistan and the Philippines. Considering that the normal pension age in the Philippines is 65 years then this shows that the average duration for pension receipt is actually only one year for men. In contrast life expectancy in Sri Lanka for women is 29 years higher than the normal retirement age of 50.

The general trend is that the non-OECD economies represented are all at the lower end of the scale with male life expectancy generally under 73 years, compared to the OECD average of 78 years, and it is over 81 years for Australia and Italy, with Hong Kong, China and Singapore also above 81. It is also noticeable that there is quite a difference in the gender gaps of life expectancy, with women as expected always being higher.

However women are only expected to live 2.1 years longer in Pakistan, whereas the difference in Viet Nam is 9.2 years. For the OECD as a whole the difference is 5.2 years with most countries having at least a four-year difference.

The second graph takes the analysis one step further as survival to age 65 is now assumed, which is the maximum normal retirement age for all but a handful of economies. Therefore the findings at this age level provide more accurate estimates of average duration for pension claimants than the previous indicators. The difference in life expectancy estimates between the highest and the lowest has reduced to six years for men and ten years for women. Although the non-OECD economies are again at the lower end the results for men are all within four years of the OECD average.

The second part of this graph is the forecast information based on 2060-65 estimates from the United Nations population database. This clearly shows that the trend in the future will be for the life expectancy gap to decrease for all non-OECD economies in comparison to the OECD average. Whilst life expectancy for the OECD countries continues to increase, it is at a much slower rate than the Asian economies. With retirement ages currently being well below 65 in many of these economies the pressures on the pension system will only increase.

Although life expectancy results are a useful tool in pension analysis they have limited use when used alone. They can provide estimates of average duration of pension receipt for those that actually begin claiming a pension, but they do not assist with providing any information about the actual numbers involved. For this population projections are required and this will now be covered in the following section.

2. RETIREMENT-INCOME INDICATORS | 35

Figure 2.7. Life expectancy at birth, in years, men and women, 2015-20

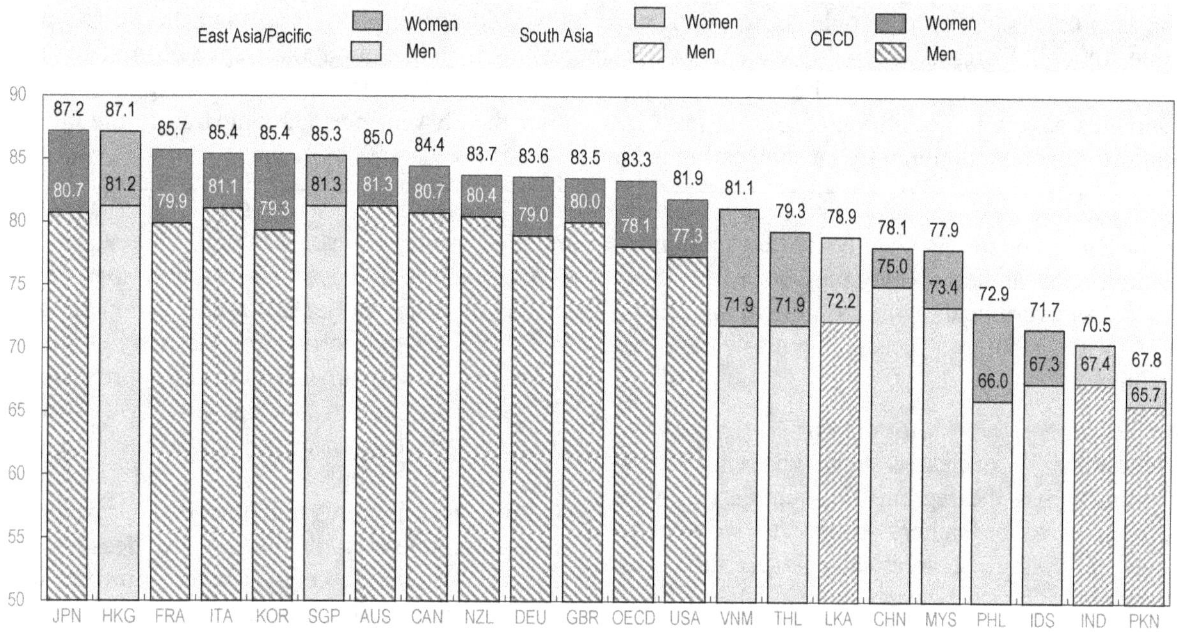

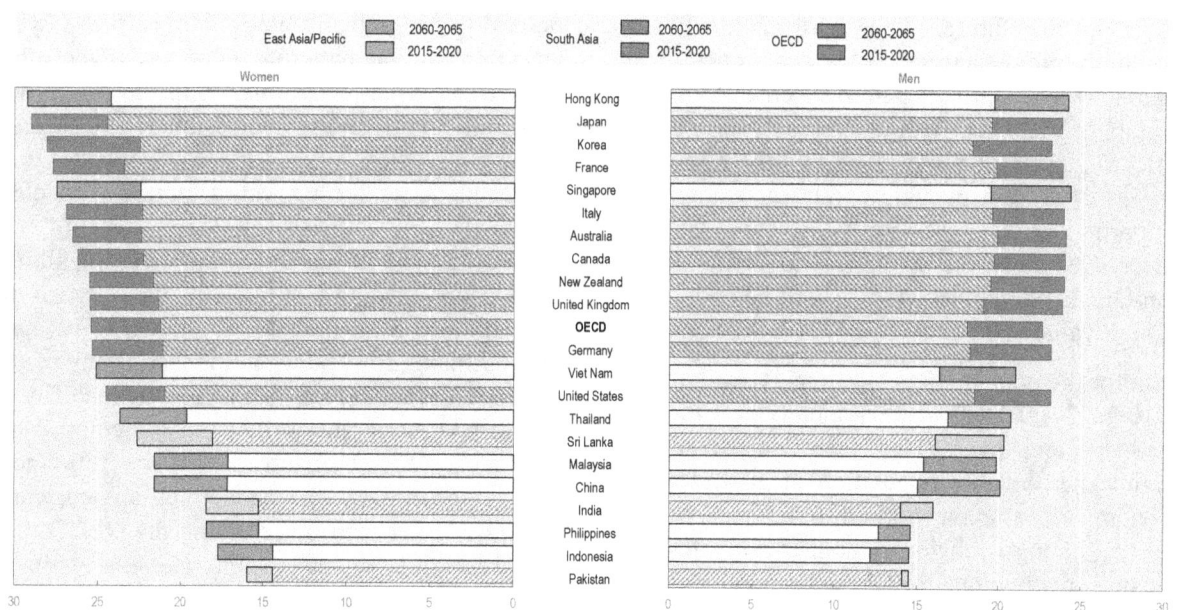

Source: United Nations, World Population Prospects – 2017 Revision.

StatLink ᔆ http://dx.doi.org/10.1787/888933873440

Figure 2.8. Life expectancy at age 65, in years, men and women, 2015-20 and 2060-65

Source: United Nations, World Population Prospects – 2017 Revision.

StatLink ᔆ http://dx.doi.org/10.1787/888933873459

Support ratio

> Asia is predicted to have a higher rate of increase in the old-age support ratio than the OECD as a whole, though Korea is a notable exception. The percentage of the population aged 65 and over in Malaysia is projected in 2100 to be about five times the level in 2015. All of the remaining non-OECD economies have a projected increase of at least 200% over the 85-year period, compared to the OECD countries which predominantly have an estimated increase of less than 100%.

Age projections are obviously a key component of any pension modelling. They enable estimation of pension costs and recipient numbers as well as providing governments with baseline assumptions upon which future pension policy can be structured.

For the support ratio information is provided for 2015 and 2055 to clearly show the trend that is apparent across the region. The summary is that the number of pensioners relative to workers is going to change dramatically over the next 40 years. As can be clearly seen all the OECD countries are already at the bottom of the graph, with the exception of Korea which is just above Hong Kong, China. However Korea is a clear example of one of the world's most rapidly ageing societies with a drop in the support ratio from 5.6 in 2015 to 1.5 in 2055, with only Japan being lower in the future. Although this decline is extremely rapid there are other economies in the region with similar patterns emerging. For example, Viet Nam will decrease from 10.4 in 2015 to 2.5 in 2055 and given that the retirement age in Viet Nam is below 60 for women the proportion of pensioners to workers will be even lower. Generally the support ratio values in the non-OECD economies in 2055 will be about 30% of their value in 2015.

Data for the population projections is available for 2010 to 2100 at five-yearly intervals for those aged 65 and over. This therefore covers the eligible pensionable population in all but a few economies that have normal retirement beyond age 65, though obviously under-estimates the pension population for those economies with earlier retirement ages.

The next two graphs show the age projection statistics, and to enable easier interpretation have been divided into OECD and Asia.

The second graph is for the OECD countries included in this report. Germany, Italy, Japan and Korea generally have the highest percentage across all the projected years, though after 2055-2065 the proportion for these economies is in decline, from estimated highs of approximately 37%-38%, for Japan and Korea and 32-34% for Germany and Italy, of the population being age 65 and over. This is only to be expected because of the lower fertility rates that have been prevalent in these economies within the last few decades. All economies generally converge at approximately 30% of their population being aged at least 65 years in 2100, with the United States slightly lower at just below 28%.

The third graph covers the non-OECD economies. An increasing elderly population is the highlight of this picture, with the proportion in Malaysia increasing more than five-fold over the 85 year period. A similar pattern occurs across the other non-OECD Asian economies with the proportion of people aged 65 and over estimated to at least treble in virtually every economy between 2015 and 2100. After the projection period it is clear that estimates indicate at least 20% of the population will be aged 65 and over in all the Asian economies. In fact by 2100 over 40% of the population in Singapore are estimated to be aged over 65 making it by far the highest of any of the countries covered. This means that the majority of non-OECD economies will be directly comparable with most OECD countries. As the retirement ages in the non-OECD economies are currently generally lower than those within the OECD then the proportion of pensioners in Asia will be considerably higher than within the OECD if the current systems remain in place.

Figure 2.9. Old-age support ratio, 2015 and 2055

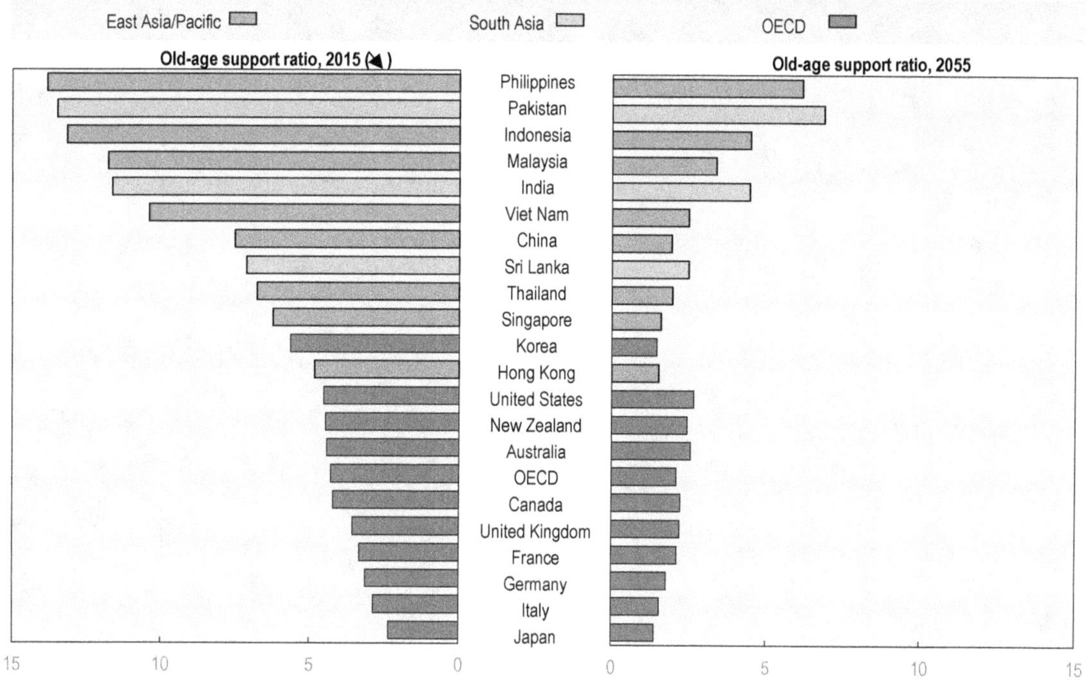

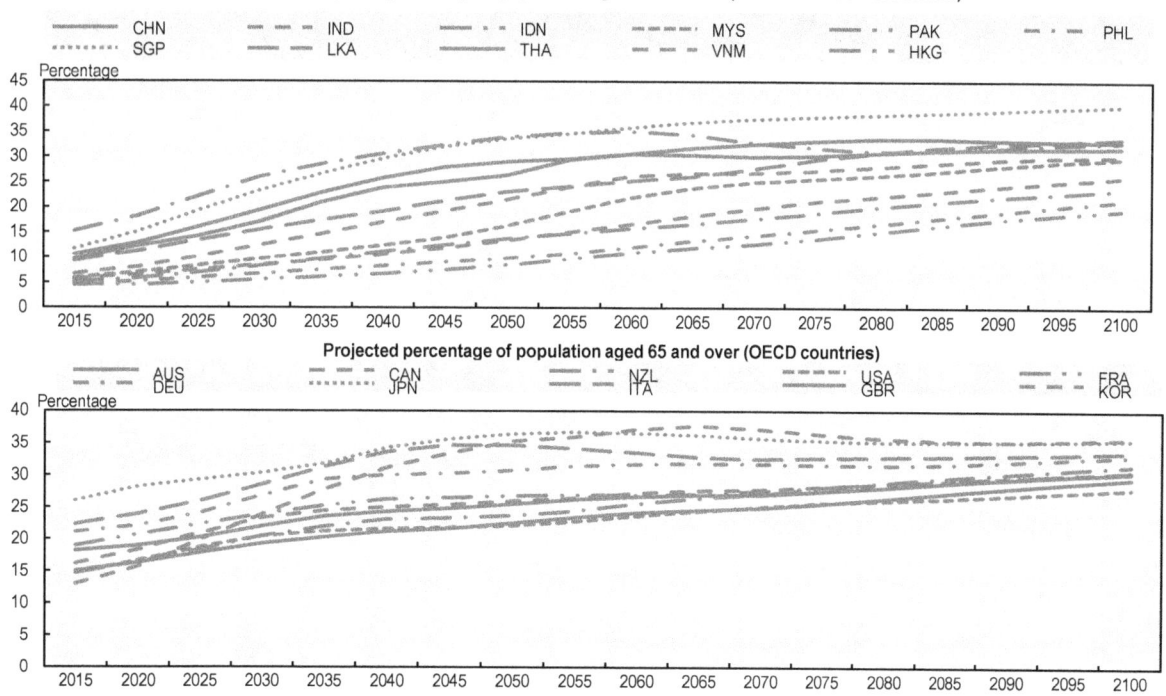

Note: The old-age support ratio is defined as the number of the population aged 15 to 64 per member of the population aged 65+.
Source: United Nations World Population Prospects, 2017 Revision.

StatLink https://dx.doi.org/10.1787/888933873478

Figure 2.10. Old-age population projections

Source: United Nations World Population Prospects, 2017 Revision.

StatLink https://dx.doi.org/10.1787/888933873497

Chapter 3. Pensions at a Glance Asia/Pacific: Pension profiles

This chapter provides detailed background information on each of the 11 non-OECD economies' retirement-income arrangements. These include pension eligibility ages and other qualifying conditions; the rules for calculating benefit entitlements; the treatment of early and late retirees. The pension profiles summarise the national results in standard charts and tables. The p for the OECD countries included can be found at http://oe.cd/pag.

Introduction

The pension profiles follow a standard schema. First, there is a detailed description of the rules and parameters of the pension schemes:

- Qualifying conditions: pension eligibility (or "retirement") age and years of contributions required to receive a pension.

- Benefit calculation: the rules for each of the schemes making up the pension system, such as earnings-related schemes, mandatory private plans and resource-tested schemes.

- Early and late retirement: the rules and conditions under which workers can retire early or continue to work beyond the standard retirement age.

- Treatment of pensioners under the personal income tax and social security contributions, including any relief for pension income.

Values of all pension parameters and other relevant figures, such as minimum wages, are given in the national currencies as a proportion of average earnings.

A summary results table gives expected relative pension values, replacement rates and pension wealth at different individual levels of earnings for mandatory pension schemes. (See Chapter 1 of this report for the definition and measurement of the different indicators.) These are given in both gross and net terms (the latter taking account of taxes and contributions paid when working and when drawing the pension).

Summary charts show the breakdown of the gross relative pension value into the different components of the pension scheme (the first row of the charts). As far as possible, the same terminology is used to describe these schemes. The particular national scheme that is described can be found in the text of the pension profile. Some standard abbreviations are used in the legends of the charts:

- SA: social assistance

- Targeted: separate resource-tested schemes for older people.

- Minimum: a minimum pension within an earnings related scheme.

- Basic: a pension based only on number of years of coverage or residency.

- Earnings-related: all public earnings-related programmes, including notional accounts and points schemes as well as traditional defined benefit plans.

- DC: defined contribution, mandatory private plans.

- Occupational: mandatory pensions, which can be provided by employers, industry-wide schemes, profession-based schemes or publicly.

The second row of charts shows the effect of personal income taxes and social security contributions on relative pension values and replacement rates, giving the gross and net values.

The charts use a standard scale to ease comparisons between economies: the scale for replacement rates runs to 125% while that for relative pension values runs to 2.5 times average earnings. In some cases, pension benefits exceed these maxima and so the measure has been capped at these levels.

China

China: Pension system in 2016

China has a two component pension system, consisting of a defined benefit earnings-related pension and a mandatory defined contribution scheme. It covers urban workers and many of the parameters depend on province-wide (rather than national) average earnings.

Key indicators: China

		China	OECD
Average earnings	CNY	67 569	254 329
	USD	9 730	36 622
Public pension spending	% of GDP	4.3	8.2
Life expectancy	at birth	76.5	80.9
	at age 65	16.1	19.7
Population over age 65	% of working- age population	13.3	23.4

StatLink http://dx.doi.org/10.1787/888933873516

Qualifying conditions

Normal pension age is 60 years for men, 50 years for blue collar women and 55 years for white collar women.

Benefit calculation

Earnings-related

The pension pays 1% of the average of the indexed individual wage and the province-wide average earnings for each year of coverage, subject to a minimum of 15 years of contributions. The pension in payment is indexed to a mix of wages and prices, which has been about 6% in recent years. The modelling assumes 50% indexation to wages.

Defined contribution (funded or notional accounts)

The second system comprises individual accounts. In addition to the north-eastern provinces (Liaoning, Jilin and Heilongjiang), a further eight have funded individual account systems. In other cases, the accounts are largely notional and are credited with a notional interest rate.

Employees pay 8% of wages to the individual account system. The accumulated balance in the fund or the notional account is converted into a stream of pension payments at the time of retirement by dividing the balance by a government-determined annuity factor, depending on individual retirement age and average national life expectancy. In all provinces, these annuity factors, for both males and females, (for monthly benefits) are:

Age	40	45	50	55	60	65	70
Factor	233	216	195	170	139	101	56

Variant careers

Early retirement

It is possible to claim a pension benefit from the age of 55 years for men and 50 years for women if the individual engaged in physical work in certain industries or posts.

Late retirement

It is possible to defer pension payments until after normal pension age, but the pension benefit is not valorised.

Personal income tax and social security contributions

Taxation of workers

There is a standard income-tax allowance of CNY 42 000. Employees are allowed to deduct social insurance and housing fund contributions to calculate taxable income.

Taxation of worker's income

Grade	Monthly taxable income	Tax-rate (%)
1	Less than CNY 1 500	3
2	The portion of income in excess of CNY 1 500 to CNY 4 500	10
3	The portion of income in excess of CNY 4 500 to CNY 9 000	20
4	The portion of income in excess of CNY 9 000 to CNY 35 000	25
5	The portion of income in excess of CNY 35 000 to CNY 55 000	30
6	The portion of income in excess of CNY 55 000 to CNY 80 000	35
7	The portion of income in excess of CNY 80 000	45

Note: "Monthly taxable income" mentioned in this schedule refers to the amount remaining from the gross income in a month after the deduction of CNY 3 500.

Social security contributions payable by workers

Under the revised system, employers contribute a maximum of 20% of earnings to cover the earnings-related pension. The second-tier pension is financed by an 8% contribution from employees. These contributions are capped at three times the local average wage. The social security contributions to individual accounts are exempt from income taxes.

Taxation of pensioners

There is no additional tax relief for pensioners.

Social security contributions payable by pensioners

Pensioners do not pay any social security contributions.

Pension modelling results: China in 2056 retirement at age 60 (men)

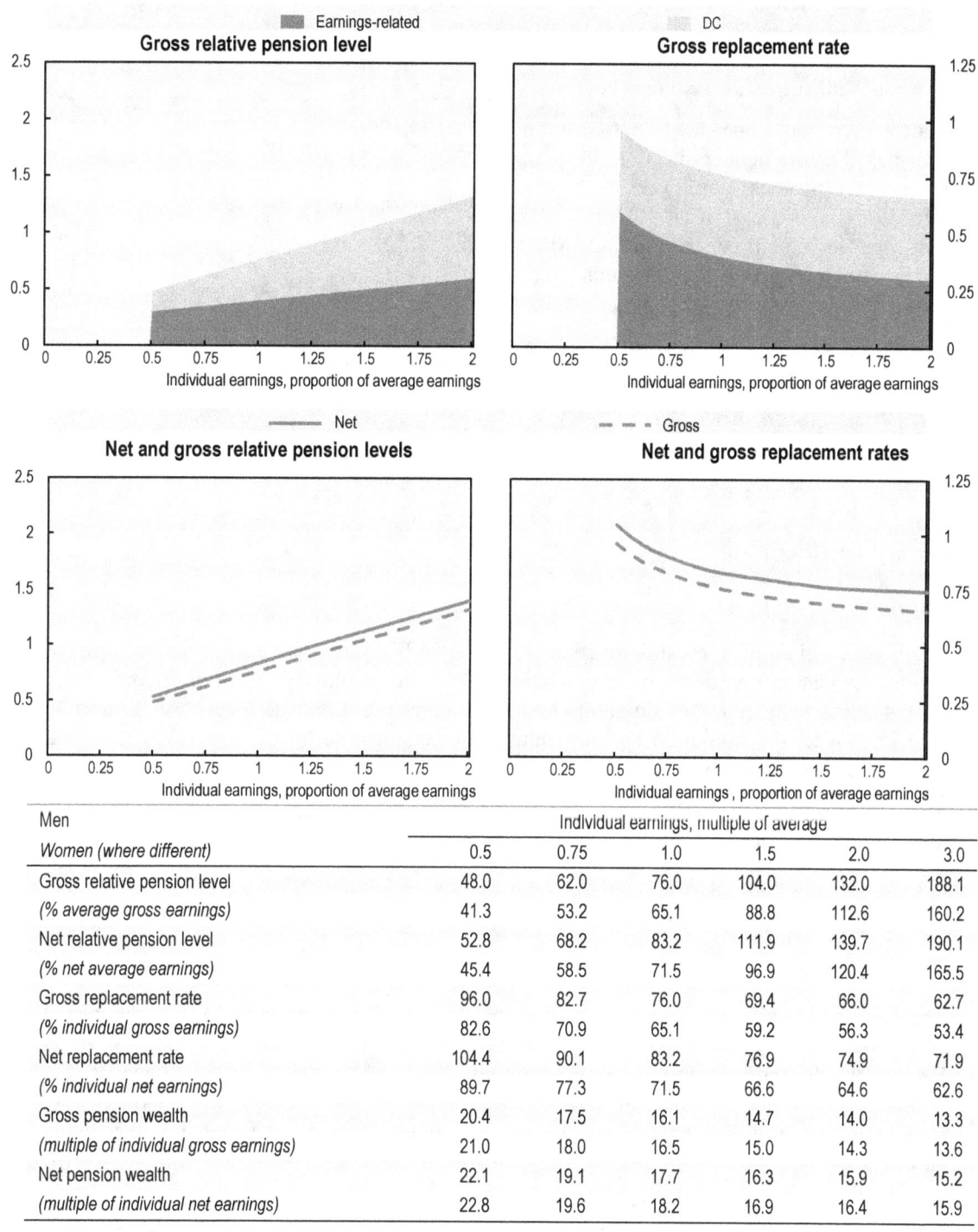

Men	Individual earnings, multiple of average					
Women (where different)	0.5	0.75	1.0	1.5	2.0	3.0
Gross relative pension level	48.0	62.0	76.0	104.0	132.0	188.1
(% average gross earnings)	41.3	53.2	65.1	88.8	112.6	160.2
Net relative pension level	52.8	68.2	83.2	111.9	139.7	190.1
(% net average earnings)	45.4	58.5	71.5	96.9	120.4	165.5
Gross replacement rate	96.0	82.7	76.0	69.4	66.0	62.7
(% individual gross earnings)	82.6	70.9	65.1	59.2	56.3	53.4
Net replacement rate	104.4	90.1	83.2	76.9	74.9	71.9
(% individual net earnings)	89.7	77.3	71.5	66.6	64.6	62.6
Gross pension wealth	20.4	17.5	16.1	14.7	14.0	13.3
(multiple of individual gross earnings)	21.0	18.0	16.5	15.0	14.3	13.6
Net pension wealth	22.1	19.1	17.7	16.3	15.9	15.2
(multiple of individual net earnings)	22.8	19.6	18.2	16.9	16.4	15.9

Assumptions: Real rate of return 3%, real earnings growth 1.25%, inflation 2%, and real discount rate 2%. All systems are modelled and indexed according to what is legislated. Transitional rules apply where relevant. DC conversion rate equal 90%. Labour market entry occurs at age 20 in 2016. Tax system latest available: 2016.

StatLink http://dx.doi.org/10.1787/888933873535

Hong Kong, China

Hong Kong, China: Pension system in 2016

The Mandatory Provident Fund (MPF) system is an employment-based retirement protection system. Except for exempt persons, employees and self-employed persons who are at least 18 but under 65 years of age are required to join an MPF scheme. MPF schemes are, privately managed, fully funded defined contribution schemes.

Key indicators: Hong Kong, China

		Hong Kong, China	OECD
Average earnings	HKD	157 800	283 992
	USD	20 349	36 622
Public pension spending	% of GDP		8.2
Life expectancy	at birth	84.2	80.9
	at age 65	21.9	19.7
Population over age 65	% of working-age population	20.7	23.4

StatLink https://dx.doi.org/10.1787/888933873554

Qualifying conditions

Withdrawal of accrued benefits from the MPF System is allowed when scheme members reach the retirement age of 65.

Benefit calculation

Defined contribution

Employees and employers who are covered by the MPF System are each required to make regular mandatory contributions calculated at 5% of the employee's relevant income to an MPF scheme, subject to the minimum and maximum relevant income levels. For a monthly paid employee, the minimum and maximum relevant income levels are HKD 7 100 and HKD 30 000 respectively.

Accrued benefits in the MPF System are withdrawn in a lump sum when scheme members reach the retirement age of 65.

For comparison with other economies, for replacement rate purposes the pension is shown as a price-indexed annuity based on sex-specific mortality rates.

Targeted/Basic

The old-age allowance has two levels. Normal old age allowance (NOAA) is means-tested and provided to those between 65 and 69. For a single person, the asset limit is HKD 219 000 and monthly income limit is HKD 7 580 (after which benefits are withdrawn). Limits for married couples are higher (HKD 332 000 and HKD 12 290, respectively). The full benefit is HKD 2 495 per month, which is about 8.3% of average earnings.

Higher older age allowance (HOAA) is for those aged 70 and above. It is a basic plan paying a flat amount of HKD 1 290 per month with no claw-back. Again, there is no formal indexation rule, so the modelling assumes price indexation.

Variant careers

Early retirement

For the MPF System, it is possible to withdraw the benefits from age 60 if ceasing employment permanently. However, the targeted/basic programme does not provide benefits until 65.

Late retirement

It is possible to combine working and receiving pension. For the MPF System, upon reaching age 65, if an individual continues to work, no further mandatory contributions will be required and the individual may withdraw the benefits derived from mandatory contributions.

Personal income tax and social security contributions

Taxation of workers

Employees can claim tax deductions for their mandatory contributions made to an MPF scheme, to a maximum of HKD 18 000.

Any voluntary contributions made by employees are not tax deductible.

Taxation of worker's income

The lower of the following two tax rules are applied. The first rule is described in the following tax schedule. This is applied to taxable income (after deduction and allowance). The basic allowance for a single person in 2016 is HKD 132 000.

Annual Taxable Income (HKD)	Tax Rate
40 000	2%
40 000 – 80 000	7%
80 000 – 120 000	12%
> 120 000	17%

Social security contributions payable by workers

The information of mandatory contributions made by employees and self-employed persons to the MPF System are provided in the section of "Defined contribution".

Taxation of pensioners

There is no additional tax relief for pensioners.

Taxation of pension income

MPF benefits derived from mandatory contributions are not subject to tax on withdrawal (only lump sum withdrawal is allowed).

Social security contributions payable by pensioners

Pensioners do not pay any social security contributions.

Pension modelling results: Hong Kong, China in 2061 retirement at age 65

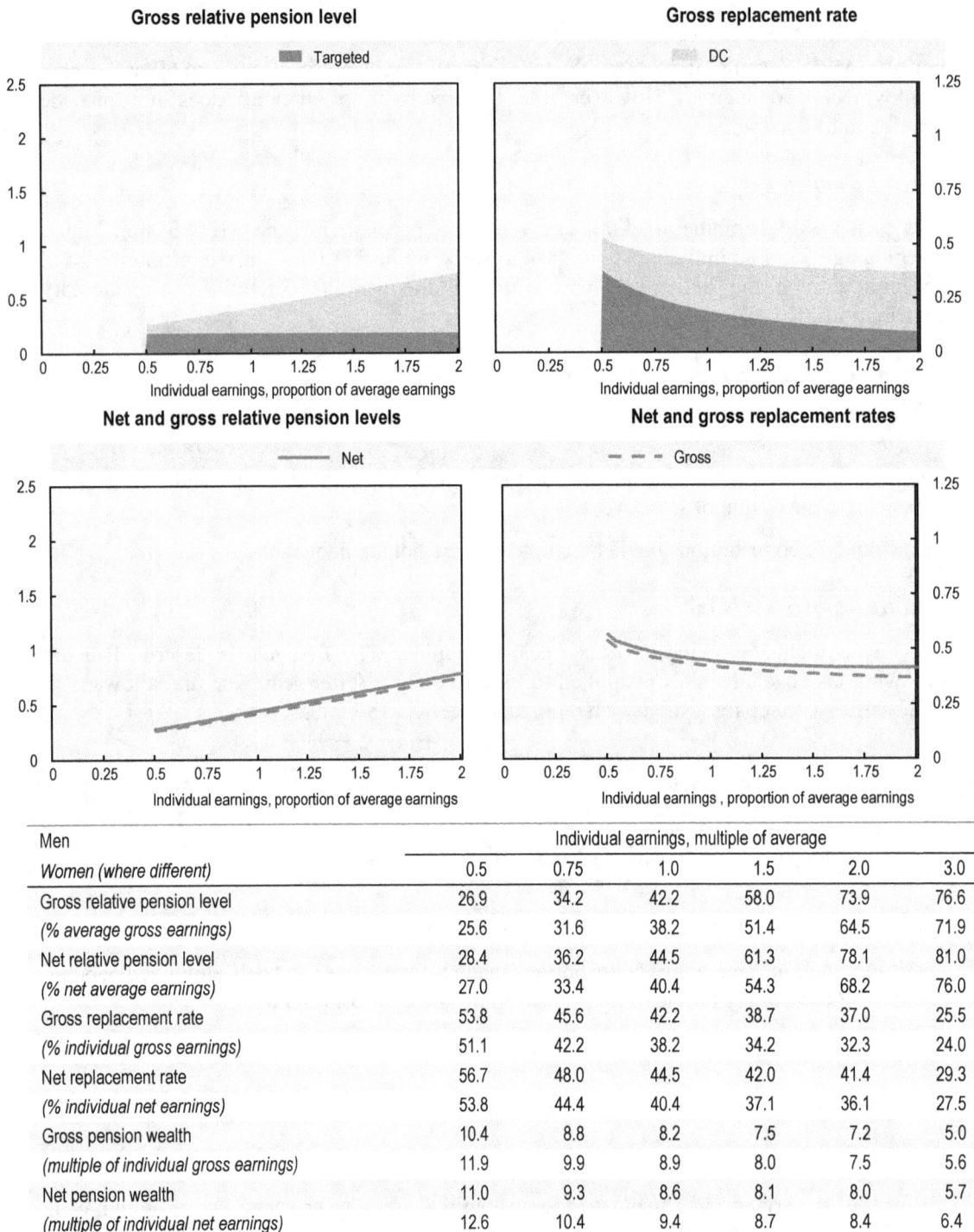

Men	Individual earnings, multiple of average					
Women (where different)	0.5	0.75	1.0	1.5	2.0	3.0
Gross relative pension level	26.9	34.2	42.2	58.0	73.9	76.6
(% average gross earnings)	25.6	31.6	38.2	51.4	64.5	71.9
Net relative pension level	28.4	36.2	44.5	61.3	78.1	81.0
(% net average earnings)	27.0	33.4	40.4	54.3	68.2	76.0
Gross replacement rate	53.8	45.6	42.2	38.7	37.0	25.5
(% individual gross earnings)	51.1	42.2	38.2	34.2	32.3	24.0
Net replacement rate	56.7	48.0	44.5	42.0	41.4	29.3
(% individual net earnings)	53.8	44.4	40.4	37.1	36.1	27.5
Gross pension wealth	10.4	8.8	8.2	7.5	7.2	5.0
(multiple of individual gross earnings)	11.9	9.9	8.9	8.0	7.5	5.6
Net pension wealth	11.0	9.3	8.6	8.1	8.0	5.7
(multiple of individual net earnings)	12.6	10.4	9.4	8.7	8.4	6.4

Assumptions: Real rate of return 3%, real earnings growth 1.25%, inflation 2%, and real discount rate 2%. All systems are modelled and indexed according to what is legislated. Transitional rules apply where relevant. DC conversion rate equal 90%. Labour market entry occurs at age 20 in 2016. Tax system latest available: 2016.

StatLink http://dx.doi.org/10.1787/888933873573

India

India: Pension system in 2016

Workers are covered under the earnings-related employee pension scheme and defined contribution employee provident fund administered by the Employees Provident Fund Organization (EPFO) and other employer managed funds.

Key indicators: India

		India	OECD
Average earnings	INR	99 349	2 489 089
	USD	1 462	36 622
Public pension spending	% of GDP		8.2
Life expectancy	at birth	69	80.9
	at age 65	14.6	19.7
Population over age 65	% of working-age population	8.6	23.4

StatLink http://dx.doi.org/10.1787/888933873592

Qualifying conditions

The normal pension age for earnings-related pension benefits from the Employees' Pension Scheme is 58 years with a minimum of 10 years of contributions. The pension age for the earnings-related Employees Provident Fund scheme is 55 years.

About 12% of the workforce (or approximately 58 million people) are covered under various pension systems according to the 2011 census. Covered individuals belong to the organized sectors and are employed by the government, government enterprises, public and private sector enterprises.

The remaining 88% of the workforce are mainly occupied in the unorganized sector (self-employed, daily wage workers, farmers etc.) and some are in the organized sector but are not mandatorily covered by the EPFO. For this share of the workforce, the Public Provident Fund (PPF) and Postal Saving Schemes have traditionally been the main long-term savings instruments but these have only catered to a relatively small section of this population.

Benefit calculation

Employees Provident Fund Schemes (EPF)

For employees with basic wages less than or equal to INR 15 000 per month, the employee contributes 12% of the monthly salary and the employer contributes 3.67%. This combined 15.67% accumulates as a lump-sum.

For employees with basic wages above INR 15 000 per month, the employee may choose to contribute based on wage of INR 15 000 per month or contribute on the higher wage amount. The employer shall contribute based on wage of INR 15 000 per month. For an International Worker, wage ceiling of 15000/- is not applicable.

For employers with less than 10 employees, the contribution rate for the employees is 10% and the employer contributes 1.67%.

There is no annuity and full accumulations are paid on retirement after attaining 55 years of age. For comparison with other economies, for replacement rate purposes the pension is shown as a price-indexed annuity based on sex-specific mortality rates.

Employees' Pension Scheme (EPS)

Starting from September 2014 new members with basic wage above INR 15 000 per month no longer have the option of contributing to the EPS. Existing participants who have until now been contributing over the earlier INR 6 500 wage cap have an option to continue contributing over the increased wage cap of INR 15 000 but they would also have to contribute the government subsidy of 1.16% on the excess amount.

For the existing and new subscribers who are within the new basic wage cap of INR 15 000, the employer contributes an amount equal to 8.33% of the basic wage to the EPS fund and the Central Government contributes a subsidy of 1.16% of the salary into the EPS. This accumulation is used to pay various pension benefits on retirement or early termination. The kind of pension a member gets under the scheme depends upon the age at which they retire and the number of years of eligible service.

Monthly pension = (pensionable salary x pensionable service)/70

The pensionable salary will be calculated on the average monthly pay for the contribution period of the last 60 months (as against 12 months earlier) preceding the date of exit from the membership. The maximum possible replacement rate is roughly 50%.

With effect from September 2014, a minimum pension level of INR 1 000 per month has been provided under the scheme. With effect from June 2016, a subscriber is permitted to defer drawing pension by up-to two years. Every year of deferment results in an increase in the pension amount by 4%. For example, if pension is drawn from age 59 years, the pension amount would be 104% of the normal pension amount and if the pension is drawn from age 60 years, the pension amount be 108.16% of the normal pension. The subscriber may also choose to continue to contribute till the age the pension withdrawal is deferred to. In this case, the enhanced pension amount shall be determined by the pension division based on a formula.

Variant careers

Early retirement

The EPS can be claimed from age 50 with 10 years of contribution and the benefits are reduced by 4% per year of early retirement, before age 58. If a member leaves his job before rendering at least 10 years of service, he is entitled to a lump-sum withdrawal benefit. The amount he can withdraw is a proportion of his monthly salary at the date of exit from employment. This proportion depends on the number of years of eligible services he has rendered. No pension is payable in cases where there is a break in service before 10 years.

In case of EPF, there are multiple scenarios, which allow for early access to the accumulation. Partial withdrawals relate to marriage, housing advance, financing life insurance policy, illness of members/family members, withdrawals are also permitted one year before retirement etc. In addition to various permitted partial withdrawals, employees can close their account and withdraw the full corpus in case they move from one employer to another or decide to retire early. No gratuity can be claimed before five years of service.

Late retirement

It is possible to delay claiming pension after normal pension age by deferring the pension by a maximum of two years as discussed in the section on EPS.

Personal income tax and social security contributions

Taxation of workers

Contributions to the provident fund and pension scheme of EPFO are allowed as deductions from income while computing one's tax liability. A total deduction up to INR 150 000 is applied to social security contributions. This limit also includes other contributions like life insurance premium and Public Provident Fund (Voluntary Scheme) among others.

Health insurance premium up to INR 15 000 is deductible (not included in the model). Transport allowance of INR 800 per month is exempted from taxation (included in the model).

Additional deduction (not included in the model): Mediclaim premium paid for parents. Maximum deduction INR 15 000. In case any of the parents covered by the Mediclaim policy is a senior citizen, deduction amount is enhanced to INR 20 000.

Taxation of worker's income

India's financial year begins in April.

The Income Tax rates are provided below. The basic Income Tax exemption limit is different for assesses under 60 years, 60-79 years and above 80 years. Higher education and secondary cess of 3% of Income Tax is applicable over and above the amount computed as Income Tax. For assesses, whose total income exceeds INR 10 million, an additional surcharge of 15% is applicable.

The following rates apply for 2016-17:

Annual income from all sources (INR)	Income tax Rates for Male and Female below 60 years	Education Cess
Up to 250 000	Nil	Nil
250 001 – 500 000	10%	3%
500 001 – 1 000 000	20%	3%
1 000 001 and above	30%	3%

Taxation of pensioners

Health insurance premium of up to INR 20 000 is deductible for senior citizens over 65 years.

Taxation of pension income

Maturity benefits on account of provident fund and pension from EPFO are fully tax exempt. Lump-sum benefits and Periodic Annuity in case of NPS are taxable when the same is received. EPFO enjoys an EEE (exempt, exempt, exempt) regime where it is tax free during contribution, growth and withdrawal phase. NPS, on the other hand is under an EET (Exempt, Exempt, Taxed) regime where maturity benefits are taxed. As NPS is still in infancy, the rule for taxation on withdrawal does not really have any impact as the withdrawal stage is still some years away even for the first set of subscribers.

The following income tax rules apply to senior citizens over age 60.

Annual income from all sources (INR)	Income tax rates for senior citizen		Education Cess
	Aged 60-80 years	Aged above 80 years	
Up to 300 000	Nil	Nil	Nil
300 001 – 500 000	10%	Nil	3%
500 001 – 1 000 000	20%	20%	3%
1 000 001 and above	30%	30%	3%

Social security contributions payable by pensioners

Pensioners do not pay any social security contributions.

Pension modelling results: India in 2054 retirement at age 58

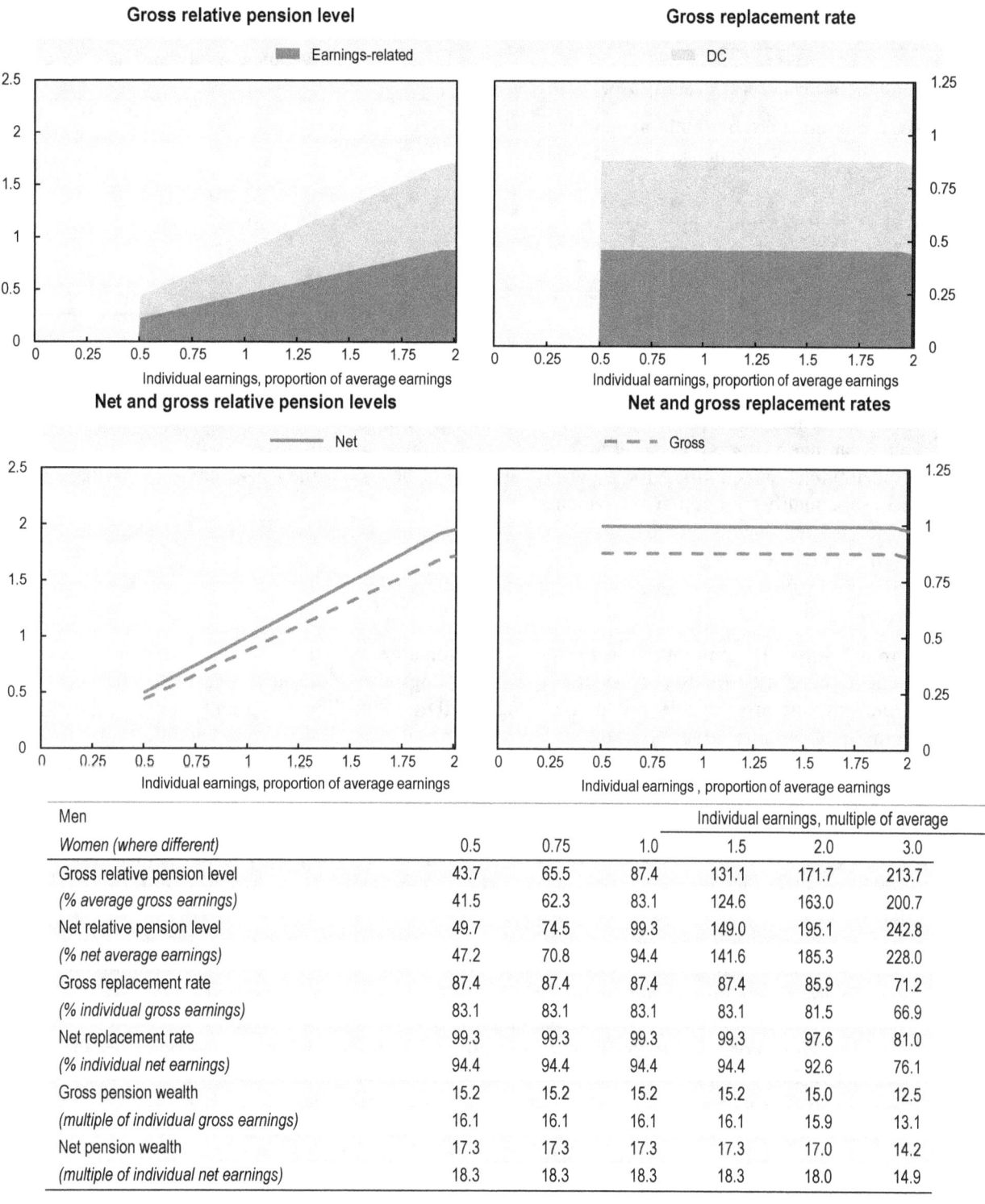

Men						
				Individual earnings, multiple of average		
Women (where different)	0.5	0.75	1.0	1.5	2.0	3.0
Gross relative pension level	43.7	65.5	87.4	131.1	171.7	213.7
(% average gross earnings)	41.5	62.3	83.1	124.6	163.0	200.7
Net relative pension level	49.7	74.5	99.3	149.0	195.1	242.8
(% net average earnings)	47.2	70.8	94.4	141.6	185.3	228.0
Gross replacement rate	87.4	87.4	87.4	87.4	85.9	71.2
(% individual gross earnings)	83.1	83.1	83.1	83.1	81.5	66.9
Net replacement rate	99.3	99.3	99.3	99.3	97.6	81.0
(% individual net earnings)	94.4	94.4	94.4	94.4	92.6	76.1
Gross pension wealth	15.2	15.2	15.2	15.2	15.0	12.5
(multiple of individual gross earnings)	16.1	16.1	16.1	16.1	15.9	13.1
Net pension wealth	17.3	17.3	17.3	17.3	17.0	14.2
(multiple of individual net earnings)	18.3	18.3	18.3	18.3	18.0	14.9

Assumptions: Real rate of return 3%, real earnings growth 1.25%, inflation 2%, and real discount rate 2%. All systems are modelled and indexed according to what is legislated. Transitional rules apply where relevant. DC conversion rate equal 90%. Labour market entry occurs at age 20 in 2016. Tax system latest available: 2016.

StatLink http://dx.doi.org/10.1787/888933873611

Indonesia

Indonesia: Pension system in 2016.

Employees are covered by both an earnings-related social insurance scheme and a defined contribution plan.

Key indicators: Indonesia

		Indonesia	OECD
Average earnings	IDR (million)	19.2	494.4
	USD	1 422	36 622
Public pension spending	% of GDP		8.2
Life expectancy	at birth	69.5	80.9
	at age 65	13.3	19.7
Population over age 65	% of working-age population	7.6	23.4

StatLink http://dx.doi.org/10.1787/888933873630

Qualifying conditions

Normal pension age is 56 years in 2016 gradually rising to 65 by 2043, increasing by one year every three years. Retirement is not required and employees with 15 years of contributions are qualified for a periodical pension benefit while those having less than 15 years qualify for lump-sum payments.

Benefit calculation

Earnings-related

From 1 July 2015 employees in the private sector are covered by social insurance. The pension benefit currently accrues at 1%. Past earnings are valorised in line with inflation. Contributions are payable up to a ceiling of IDR 7.3 million per month (2016). The minimum pension after 15 years of contribution is IDR 300 000 per month, with a maximum benefit of IDR 3.6 million per month. Pensions in payment are indexed to prices.

Defined contribution

Employees in the private sector are covered by defined contribution pension plans. From 1993 to 2013 this refers to one of the Employees Social Security Programmes (PT Jamsostek) and in this case the Jaminan Hari Tua (JHT) or Old Age Security (OAS). The JHT is a compulsory programme for all employees and the retired may opt for part lump-sum with a periodical payment until death or a full lump-sum payment. Employees contribute 2% of earnings and employers pay 3.7% of the payroll. The pension is paid as a lump sum or monthly up to a maximum of five years if the balance is more than IDR 3 million. For comparison with other economies, for replacement rate purposes the pension is shown as a price-indexed annuity based on sex-specific mortality rates.

Variant careers

Early retirement

It is possible to start claiming the pension at any age with a minimum of five years of contribution, if unemployed for at least six months.

Late retirement

The benefit may be deferred with no maximum age.

Personal income tax and social security contributions

Taxation of workers

There is a deduction of IDR 15 840 000 for a single individual. In addition, work-related expense is tax deductible and the amount is 5% of earnings up to a ceiling of IDR 6 000 000. There is also a tax deductible amount of 5% or up to IDR 2 400 000 for pension payments. Social security contributions are tax deductible.

Taxation of worker's income

Annual Income (IDR millions)	Tax Rate
Up to 50	5%
Over 50 up to 250	15%
Over 250 up to 500	25%

Social security contributions payable by workers

Employees contribute 1% of payroll to the pension plans and 1% to health care.

Taxation of pensioners

There is no additional tax relief for pensioners.

Taxation of pension income

Annual Income (IDR millions)	Tax Rate
Up to 25	Nil
Over 25 up to 50	5%
Over 50 up to 100	10%
Over 100 up to 200	15%
Over 200	25%

Social security contributions payable by pensioners

Pensioners do not pay any social security contributions.

Pension modelling results: Indonesia in 2061 retirement at age 65

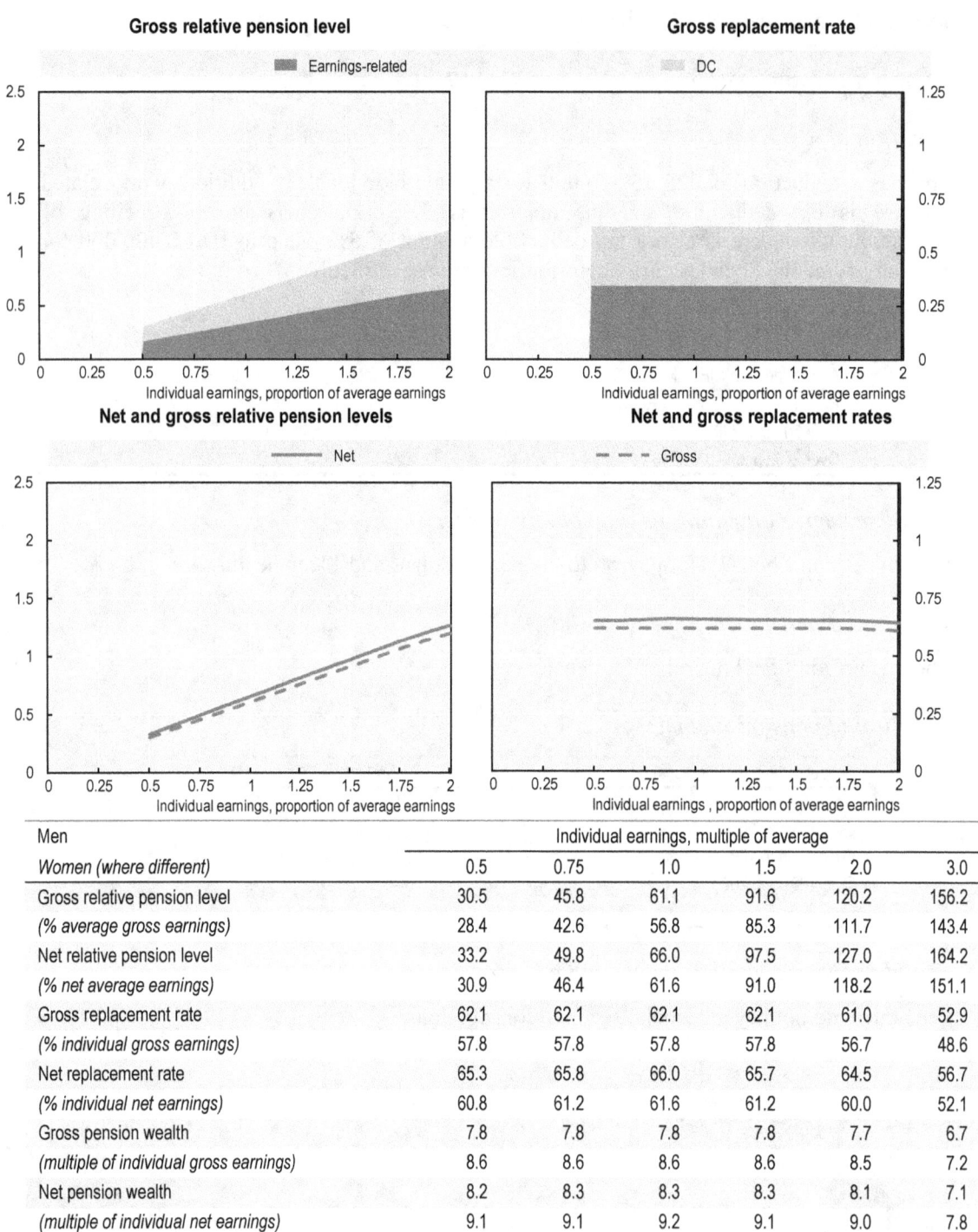

Men	Individual earnings, multiple of average					
Women (where different)	0.5	0.75	1.0	1.5	2.0	3.0
Gross relative pension level	30.5	45.8	61.1	91.6	120.2	156.2
(% average gross earnings)	28.4	42.6	56.8	85.3	111.7	143.4
Net relative pension level	33.2	49.8	66.0	97.5	127.0	164.2
(% net average earnings)	30.9	46.4	61.6	91.0	118.2	151.1
Gross replacement rate	62.1	62.1	62.1	62.1	61.0	52.9
(% individual gross earnings)	57.8	57.8	57.8	57.8	56.7	48.6
Net replacement rate	65.3	65.8	66.0	65.7	64.5	56.7
(% individual net earnings)	60.8	61.2	61.6	61.2	60.0	52.1
Gross pension wealth	7.8	7.8	7.8	7.8	7.7	6.7
(multiple of individual gross earnings)	8.6	8.6	8.6	8.6	8.5	7.2
Net pension wealth	8.2	8.3	8.3	8.3	8.1	7.1
(multiple of individual net earnings)	9.1	9.1	9.2	9.1	9.0	7.8

Assumptions: Real rate of return 3%, real earnings growth 1.25%, inflation 2%, and real discount rate 2%. All systems are modelled and indexed according to what is legislated. Transitional rules apply where relevant. DC conversion rate equal 90%. Labour market entry occurs at age 20 in 2016. Tax system latest available: 2016.

StatLink http://dx.doi.org/10.1787/888933873649

Malaysia

Malaysia: The pension system in 2016

Private sector employees and non-pensionable public sector employees contribute to the provident fund, with social assistance paid to those with insufficient income.

Key indicators: Malaysia

		Malaysia	OECD
Average earnings	MYR	83 496	164 287
	USD	18 613	36 622
Public pension spending	% of GDP	2	8.2
Life expectancy	at birth	75.6	80.9
	at age 65	16.3	19.7
Population over age 65	% of working-age population	8.5	23.4

StatLink http://dx.doi.org/10.1787/888933873668

Qualifying conditions

Funds can be withdrawn from age 55, and retirement is not necessary. Eligibility to social benefits, however, is from age 60.

Benefit calculation

Defined contribution

Employees pay 8% of monthly earnings to the provident fund according to wage classes, when aged up to age 60, and 4% between age 60 and 75. Employers pay 13% of monthly earnings according to wage classes for employees up to 60 years of age and earning under RM 5 000 per month, and 12% for earnings above RM 5 000 per month. Employer contributions are 6.5% and 6% respectively, between ages 60 and 75, for those earning under and above RM 5 000 per month. Minimum monthly earnings for the contribution are MYR 10 and there is no ceiling for the contribution. Insured persons can make voluntary additional contributions.

The contribution is made to two different accounts: 70% of contribution to Account 1 and 30% to Account 2. It is possible to receive pension in a lump sum, monthly instalments or a combination of both. The minimum total amount to be paid in monthly instalments is RM 250 with the minimum period being 12 months, with a minimum withdrawal at any time of at least MYR 2 000, or a combination of these options. For comparison with other economies, for replacement rate purposes the pension is shown as a price-indexed annuity based on sex-specific mortality rates.

The guaranteed minimum interest rate is 2.5% a year. If funds remain in the accounts after age 55, fund members continue to earn compound interest until age 100.

Old-age assistance

A monthly benefit of RM 300 is paid to those aged 60 and assessed as needy (below poverty line), with no financial support from other family members.

Variant careers

Early retirement

It is possible to make a one-time withdrawal of savings at age 50 from Account 2.

Late retirement

It is possible to defer retirement and continue to make contributions after normal pension age.

Personal income tax and social security contributions

Taxation of workers

The mandatory and voluntary provident fund contributions up to RM 6 000 a month are tax deductible. Employees below age 55 earning RM 3 000 or less a month and casual workers need to be covered by social insurance. The insurance does not cover old-age pension, but disability, survivor and other pensions and grants. The contribution rate is 0.5% of monthly earnings for employees and 1.75%.

Taxation of worker's income

Chargeable Income	MYR	Rate	Tax (MYR)
On the first	5 000	0%	0
On the next	15 000	1%	150
On the next	15 000	5%	750
On the next	15 000	10%	1 500
On the next	20 000	16%	3 200
On the next	30 000	21%	6 300
On the next	150 000	24%	36 000
On the next	150 000	24.5%	36 750
On the next	200 000	25%	50 000
On the next	400 000	26%	104 000
Exceeding	1 000 000	28%	-

Social security contributions payable by workers

Workers make contributions as described above.

Taxation of pensioners

There is no additional tax relief for pensioners.

Taxation of pension income

Pension income is tax exempted.

Social security contributions payable by pensioners

Pensioners do not pay any social security contributions.

Pension modelling results: Malaysia in 2051 retirement at age 55

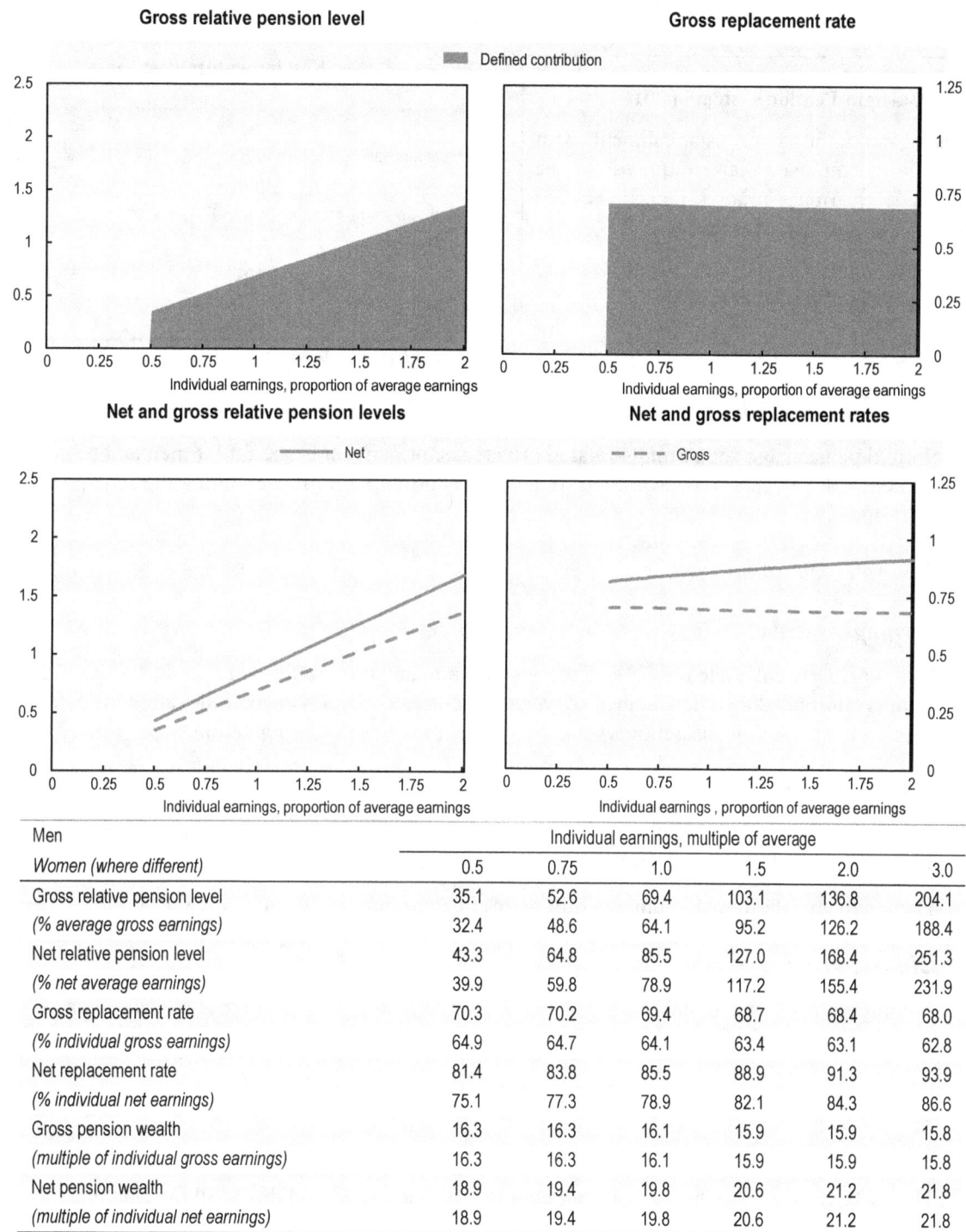

Men	Individual earnings, multiple of average					
Women (where different)	0.5	0.75	1.0	1.5	2.0	3.0
Gross relative pension level	35.1	52.6	69.4	103.1	136.8	204.1
(% average gross earnings)	32.4	48.6	64.1	95.2	126.2	188.4
Net relative pension level	43.3	64.8	85.5	127.0	168.4	251.3
(% net average earnings)	39.9	59.8	78.9	117.2	155.4	231.9
Gross replacement rate	70.3	70.2	69.4	68.7	68.4	68.0
(% individual gross earnings)	64.9	64.7	64.1	63.4	63.1	62.8
Net replacement rate	81.4	83.8	85.5	88.9	91.3	93.9
(% individual net earnings)	75.1	77.3	78.9	82.1	84.3	86.6
Gross pension wealth	16.3	16.3	16.1	15.9	15.9	15.8
(multiple of individual gross earnings)	16.3	16.3	16.1	15.9	15.9	15.8
Net pension wealth	18.9	19.4	19.8	20.6	21.2	21.8
(multiple of individual net earnings)	18.9	19.4	19.8	20.6	21.2	21.8

Assumptions: Real rate of return 3%, real earnings growth 1.25%, inflation 2%, and real discount rate 2%. All systems are modelled and indexed according to what is legislated. Transitional rules apply where relevant. DC conversion rate equal 90%. Labour market entry occurs at age 20 in 2016. Tax system latest available: 2016.

StatLink http://dx.doi.org/10.1787/888933873687

Pakistan

Pakistan: Pension system in 2016

Workers of an industry or establishment with five or more employees are required to be insured under earnings-related pension called employees' old-age benefit scheme.

The model assumes that workers are covered by the earnings-related pension (EOBI).

Key indicators: Pakistan

		Pakistan	OECD
Average earnings	PKR	160 280	3 819 683
	USD	1 537	36 622
Public pension spending	% of GDP	0.5	8.2
Life expectancy	at birth	66.7	80.9
	at age 65	14.3	19.7
Population over age 65	% of working-age population	7.4	23.4

StatLink https://dx.doi.org/10.1787/888933873706

Qualifying conditions

Normal pension age for earnings-related private sector pension is age 60 for men and 55 for women with 15 years of contribution (relaxation is provided for those joining the scheme at older ages).

Benefit calculation

Earnings-related

The pension is calculated as 2% of the insured's average monthly earnings in the last 12 months multiplied by the number of years of covered employment. Indexation rule for pension in payment is discretionary and the model assumes price-indexation.

Minimum pension

Minimum pension is PKR 5 250 per month. Indexation for pension in payment is discretionary and the model assumes price-indexation.

The amount of (both maximum and minimum) insured monthly wage is PKR 15 000.

Old-age grant

A lump sum of one month of the insured's average monthly earnings for each year of contributions is paid for those with at least two but fewer than 15 years of contributions.

Variant careers

Early retirement

The earliest age at which men can start claiming pension is 55 and this is 50 for women.

The reduction applied is 0.5% for each completed month by which age at retirement falls short of 60 (55 years for women). This reduction is also applicable to the minimum pension.

Late retirement

It is possible to start receiving pension after normal pension age.

Personal income tax and social security contributions

Taxation of workers

Taxable Income in PKR	Rate of Tax
0 to 400 000	0%
400 000 to 500 000	2% of the amount exceeding 400 000
500 000 to 750 000	2 000 + 5% of the amount exceeding 500 000
750 000 to 1 400 000	14 500 + 10% of the amount exceeding 750 000
1 400 000 to 1 500 000	79 500 + 12.5% of the amount exceeding 1 400 000
1 500 000 to 1 800 000	92 000 + 15% of the amount exceeding 1 500 000
1 800 000 to 2 500 000	137 000 + 17.5% of the amount exceeding 1 800 000
2 500 000 to 3 000 000	259 500 + 20% of the amount exceeding 2 500 000
3 000 000 to 3 500 000	359 500 + 22.5% of the amount exceeding 3 000 000
3 500 000 to 4 000 000	472 000 + 25% of the amount exceeding 3 500 000
4 000 000 to 7 000 000	597 000 + 27.5% of the amount exceeding 4 000 000
7 000 000 and above	1 422 000 + 30% of the amount exceeding 7 000 000

Social security contributions payable by workers

Employer pays 5% of the minimum wage (PKR 15 000) and employee pays contribution at the rate of 1% of minimum wage.

Taxation of pensioners

The additional tax relief for older people is 50% for taxable income less than or equal to PKR 1000 000.

Taxation of pension income

All benefits received from the EOBI on retirement or death are not taxed. Lump-sum benefit from Voluntary Pension System is exempt however, pension payments are taxed.

Social security contributions payable by pensioners

Pensioners do not pay any social security contributions.

Pension modelling results: Pakistan in 2056 retirement at age 60 (men)

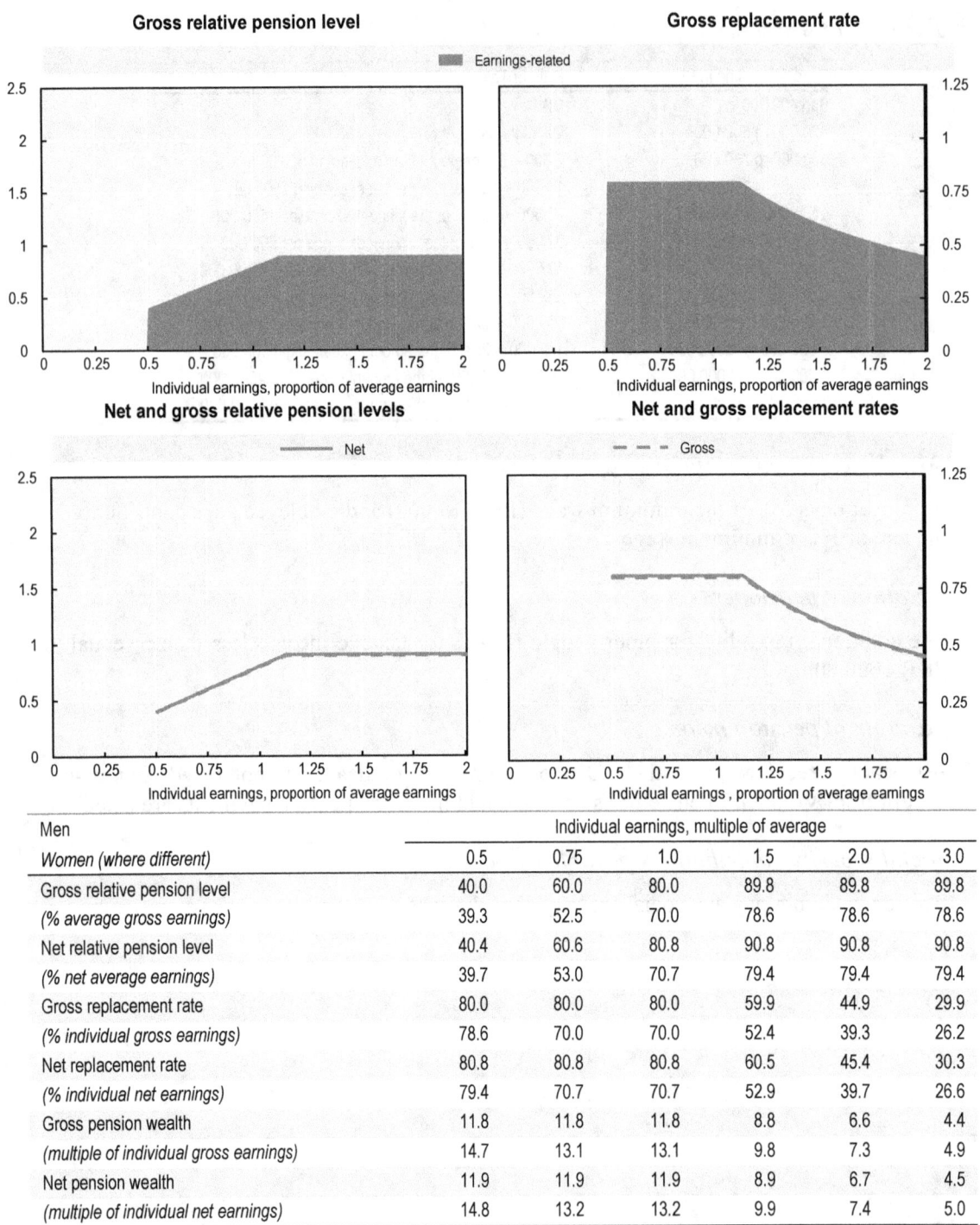

Men	Individual earnings, multiple of average					
Women (where different)	0.5	0.75	1.0	1.5	2.0	3.0
Gross relative pension level	40.0	60.0	80.0	89.8	89.8	89.8
(% average gross earnings)	39.3	52.5	70.0	78.6	78.6	78.6
Net relative pension level	40.4	60.6	80.8	90.8	90.8	90.8
(% net average earnings)	39.7	53.0	70.7	79.4	79.4	79.4
Gross replacement rate	80.0	80.0	80.0	59.9	44.9	29.9
(% individual gross earnings)	78.6	70.0	70.0	52.4	39.3	26.2
Net replacement rate	80.8	80.8	80.8	60.5	45.4	30.3
(% individual net earnings)	79.4	70.7	70.7	52.9	39.7	26.6
Gross pension wealth	11.8	11.8	11.8	8.8	6.6	4.4
(multiple of individual gross earnings)	14.7	13.1	13.1	9.8	7.3	4.9
Net pension wealth	11.9	11.9	11.9	8.9	6.7	4.5
(multiple of individual net earnings)	14.8	13.2	13.2	9.9	7.4	5.0

Assumptions: Real rate of return 3%, real earnings growth 1.25%, inflation 2%, and real discount rate 2%. All systems are modelled and indexed according to what is legislated. Transitional rules apply where relevant. DC conversion rate equal 90%. Labour market entry occurs at age 20 in 2016. Tax system latest available: 2016.

StatLink http://dx.doi.org/10.1787/888933873725

Philippines

Philippines: Pension system in 2016

Employees up to age 60 earning more than PHP 1 000 a month are covered by the basic, earnings-related and minimum pensions. There are special systems for government employees and military personnel.

Key indicators: Philippines

		Philippines	OECD
Average earnings	PHP	107 399	1 816 675
	USD	2 165	36 622
Public pension spending	% of GDP	1.7	8.2
Life expectancy	at birth	69.5	80.9
	at age 65	14	19.7
Population over age 65	% of working-age population	7.2	23.4

StatLink http://dx.doi.org/10.1787/888933873744

Qualifying conditions

Normal pension age is 65 with 120 months of contribution.

Benefit calculation

Basic

The monthly basic pension is PHP 300.

All pension payment is made 13 times per year in the Philippines. Indexation rule for all pension payment is decided periodically based on price inflation and wage growth and on the financial state of the fund. In a long run, it is assumed that this ad hoc adjustment will be in line with price inflation.

Earnings-related

Earnings-related pension benefit depends on the greater of the following two average earnings: the average earnings over five years at six months prior to pension claim or the average earnings for the period in which contribution was paid. The benefit is the highest of the basic pension plus 20% of workers' average monthly earnings plus 2% of workers' average monthly earnings for each year of service exceeding 10 years or 40% of the workers' average monthly earnings, whichever is greater.

Minimum

The minimum pension for both basic and earnings-related components is PHP 1 200 a month with a contribution period of between 10 years and 20 years and PHP 2 400 for more than 20 years of contribution.

Variant careers

Early retirement

People could start receiving pension as early as age 60 with 120 months of contributions at six months before retirement. The pension is suspended if an old-age pensioner resumes employment or self-employment before age 65.

Late retirement

People can start claiming pension later than normal pension age, but there is no increment for the delayed pension benefits.

Personal income tax and social security contributions

Taxation of worker's income

For resident individuals, income tax rates and bands are as follows for 2016:

Over	But Not Over	Rate
	PHP 250 000	0%
PHP 250 000	PHP 400 000	20% of the excess over PHP 250 000
PHP 400 000	PHP 800 000	PHP 30 000 + 25% of the excess over PHP 400 000
PHP 800 000	PHP 2 000 000	PHP 130 000 + 30% of the excess over PHP 800 000
PHP 2 000 000	PHP 8 000 000	PHP 490 000 + 32% of the excess over PHP 2 000 000
PHP 8 000 000		PHP 2 410 000 + 35% of the excess over PHP 8 000 000

Social security contributions payable by workers

Workers pay 4.13% of monthly gross insured earnings as social security contribution for pension, sickness and maternity and funeral benefits and the gross insured earnings are set based on 31 income classes. The maximum insured monthly earnings for contribution are PHP 16 000.

Taxation of pensioners

Under the Expanded Senior Citizens Act of 2003, senior citizens (resident citizens of the Philippines at least 60 years old) are exempted from paying individual income taxes provided their annual taxable income does not exceed the poverty level as determined by the National Economic and Development Authority (NEDA) for that year. They are also entitled to a 20% discount on the price of some services and products, including medical services and medicines. The 20% discount then becomes a tax credit for the establishment concerned.

Taxation of pension income

All pension incomes are exempt from taxation.

Social security contributions payable by pensioners

Pensioners do not pay any social security contributions.

Pension modelling results: Philippines in 2061 retirement at age 65

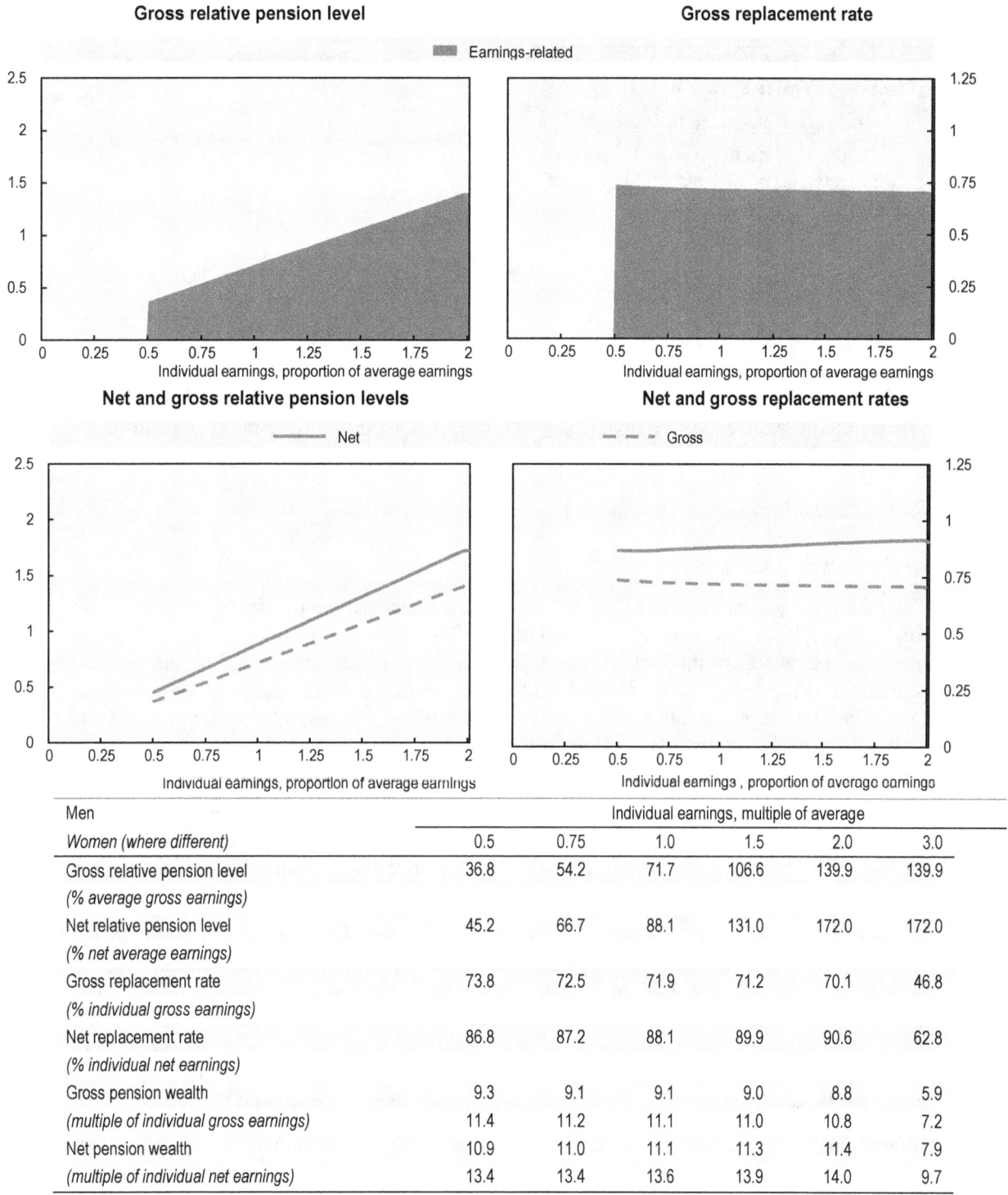

Men	Individual earnings, multiple of average					
Women (where different)	0.5	0.75	1.0	1.5	2.0	3.0
Gross relative pension level	36.8	54.2	71.7	106.6	139.9	139.9
(% average gross earnings)						
Net relative pension level	45.2	66.7	88.1	131.0	172.0	172.0
(% net average earnings)						
Gross replacement rate	73.8	72.5	71.9	71.2	70.1	46.8
(% individual gross earnings)						
Net replacement rate	86.8	87.2	88.1	89.9	90.6	62.8
(% individual net earnings)						
Gross pension wealth	9.3	9.1	9.1	9.0	8.8	5.9
(multiple of individual gross earnings)	11.4	11.2	11.1	11.0	10.8	7.2
Net pension wealth	10.9	11.0	11.1	11.3	11.4	7.9
(multiple of individual net earnings)	13.4	13.4	13.6	13.9	14.0	9.7

Assumptions: Real rate of return 3%, real earnings growth 1.25%, inflation 2%, and real discount rate 2%. All systems are modelled and indexed according to what is legislated. Transitional rules apply where relevant. DC conversion rate equal 90%. Labour market entry occurs at age 20 in 2016. Tax system latest available: 2016.

StatLink http://dx.doi.org/10.1787/888933873763

Singapore

Singapore: Pension system in 2016

The Central Provident Fund (CPF) covers all Singaporean and permanent resident workers earning a monthly wage of at least SGD 50. CPF is a defined contribution scheme.

Key indicators: Singapore

		Singapore	OECD
Average earnings	SGD	60 888	53 003
	USD	42 070	36 622
Public pension spending	% of GDP		8.2
Life expectancy	at birth	83.3	80.9
	at age 65	21.0	19.7
Population over age 65	% of working-age population	16.0	23.4

StatLink http://dx.doi.org/10.1787/888933873782

Qualifying conditions

The minimum age to start receiving payouts from the national life annuity scheme is 64 (will be 65 in 2019).

Benefit calculation

Defined contribution

The maximum contribution is calculated based on a salary ceiling of SGD 6 000 per month for both employer and employee contributions. The contribution rates vary with age as indicated below. Contributions to the Ordinary Account and Special Account are for retirement, while contributions to the MediSave Account are for medical expenses. Savings in the Ordinary Account can also be used to buy a home but amounts withdrawn must be refunded with interest upon sale of the property.

Currently savings in the Ordinary Account earn an interest rate of 2.5% per annum while savings in the other accounts earn an interest rate of 4% per annum. An extra interest of 1% per annum is paid on the first SGD 60 000 of an individual's CPF savings regardless of age. On top of this extra interest, an additional extra interest of 1% per annum is also paid on the first SGD 30 000 of CPF savings for those age 55 and above.

At age 55, savings in the Ordinary Account and Special Account are set aside in the Retirement Account to meet a specified sum. Savings above the specified sum can be withdrawn in a lump sum. Individuals who own their own homes may choose to set aside a smaller specified sum called the 'Basic Retirement Sum' (SGD 83 000 in 2017). Those who do not own their own homes need to set aside at least a 'Full Retirement Sum' (SGD 166 000 in 2017). There is also an 'Enhanced Retirement Sum' (SGD 249 000 in 2017) for those who wish to set aside a larger specified sum for retirement.

Monies in the Retirement Account are used to purchase a life annuity for the member. Monthly payouts commence from age 64 (65 in 2019), but members can start payouts later, up to age 70, for higher monthly payouts.

As the amount of Ordinary Account savings the individual uses to buy a home would affect the total amount of savings used to purchase the life annuity and in turn the benefits he receives, we lay out two scenarios, where the Ordinary Account contributes 35% and 50% to retirement benefits respectively.

In addition to the CPF retirement benefits, Singaporeans aged 65 and above who have low lifetime incomes and little to no family support receive a quarterly income supplement of SGD 300 to SGD 750 through the Silver Support Scheme.

For the purposes of comparing replacement rates with other economies, this report uses a standardized set of macro assumptions and computes the pension payout as a price-indexed annuity based on sex-specific mortality rates. The results would thus differ from that of an earlier study by academics from the National University of Singapore.

The study, which took into account institutional features unique to Singapore, found that a male entrant to the workforce earning the median income would have a net income replacement rate of 70% upon retirement at age 65. For the female entrant, the net income replacement rate was 64%.

Employee age (years)	Contribution rate (for monthly wages > SGD 1 500)			Credited to		
	Contribution by employer (% of wage)	Contribution by employee (% of wage)	Total contribution (% of wage)	Ordinary account (% of wage)	Special account (% of wage)	Medisave account (% of wage)
35 and below	17	20	37	23	6	8
Above 35-45	17	20	37	21	7	9
Above 45-50	17	20	37	19	8	10
Above 50-55	17	20	37	15	11.5	10.5
Above 55-60	13	13	26	12	3.5	10.5
Above 60-65	9	7.5	16.5	3.5	2.5	10.5
Above 65	7.5	5	12.5	1	1	10.5

Variant careers

The minimum retirement age in Singapore is age 62, but employers must offer re-employment to eligible employees who turn 62, up to age 67.

Early retirement

Individuals can make lump sum withdrawals of their CPF savings in excess of the specified sum from age 55.

Late retirement

Individuals have the option to defer the start of their life annuity payouts up to age 70 and by doing so, receive permanently higher payouts. Individuals can receive payouts from CPF while continuing to work.

Personal income tax and social security contributions

Taxation of workers

Compulsory CPF contributions are fully tax-exempt. Individuals can also receive tax relief of up to SGD 7 000 per year for voluntary contributions made by their employers or themselves to their own CPF Special or Retirement Accounts, and an additional tax relief of up to SGD 7 000 per year for voluntary contributions that they make to their family members' CPF Special or Retirement Accounts.

Taxation of worker's income

There is also tax deductible "earned income relief", and the relief amount depends on the worker's age as described below

Age	Relief amount
Below 55 years old	SGD 1 000
55 to 59 years old	SGD 6 000
60 years old and above	SGD 8 000

Individuals who wish to save more for their old age can participate in the Supplementary Retirement Scheme (SRS), a scheme operated by the private sector. SRS contributions are voluntary, and are eligible for tax relief. SRS contributions for Singaporeans and foreigners are capped at SGD15 300 and SGD35 700 respectively. SRS investment returns are accumulated tax-free and only 50% of the withdrawals from SRS are taxable at retirement.

Chargeable income	Rate (%)
Up to SGD 20 000	0
Over SGD 20 000 up to SGD 30 000	2
Over SGD 30 000 up to SGD 40 000	3.5
Over SGD 40 000 up to SGD 80 000	7
Over SGD 80 000 up to SGD 120 000	11.5
Over SGD 120 000 up to SGD 160 000	15
Over SGD 160 000 up to SGD 200 000	18
Over SGD 200 000 up to SGD 240 000	19
Over SGD 240 000 up to SGD 280 000	19.5
Over SGD 280 000 up to SGD 320 000	20
Over SGD 320 000	22

Social security contributions payable by workers

Workers make contributions to the CPF as described above.

Taxation of pensioners

There is no additional tax relief for pensioners.

Taxation of pension income

Retirement income from CPF is exempted from personal income tax.

Pensions from approved pension schemes may be taxed. The amount of pension accrued up to 31 Dec 1992 in the approved funds in Singapore is exempt from tax if the person retired at the retirement age stated in the pension or provident funds/schemes.

Pensions paid out of contributions made to the funds after 31 Dec 1992 will be taxed.

Social security contributions payable by pensioners

Individuals who work while receiving retirement income from CPF continue to make CPF contributions.

Pension modelling results: Singapore in 2061 retirement at age 65
(Ordinary Account contributes 35% of retirement benefits)

Men	Individual earnings, multiple of average					
Women (where different)	0.5	0.75	1.0	1.5	2.0	3.0
Gross relative pension level	26.6	39.8	53.1	62.9	62.9	62.9
(% average gross earnings)	23.6	35.5	47.3	56.0	56.0	56.0
Net relative pension level	29.3	43.9	58.6	69.4	69.4	69.4
(% net average earnings)	26.1	39.1	52.2	61.8	61.8	61.8
Gross replacement rate	53.1	53.1	53.1	42.0	31.5	21.0
(% individual gross earnings)	47.3	47.3	47.3	37.4	28.0	18.7
Net replacement rate	57.4	57.9	58.6	46.3	34.9	23.7
(% individual net earnings)	51.1	51.5	52.2	41.2	31.1	21.1
Gross pension wealth	10.4	10.4	10.4	8.2	6.1	4.1
(multiple of individual gross earnings)	10.4	10.4	10.4	8.2	6.1	4.1
Net pension wealth	11.2	11.3	11.4	9.0	6.8	4.6
(multiple of individual net earnings)	11.2	11.3	11.4	9.0	6.8	4.6

Assumptions: Real rate of return 3%, real earnings growth 1.25%, inflation 2%, and real discount rate 2%. All systems are modelled and indexed according to what is legislated. Transitional rules apply where relevant. DC conversion rate equal 90%. Labour market entry occurs at age 20 in 2016. Tax system latest available: 2016.

StatLink http://dx.doi.org/10.1787/888933873801

Pension modelling results: Singapore in 2061 retirement at age 65
(Ordinary Account contributes 50% of retirement benefits)

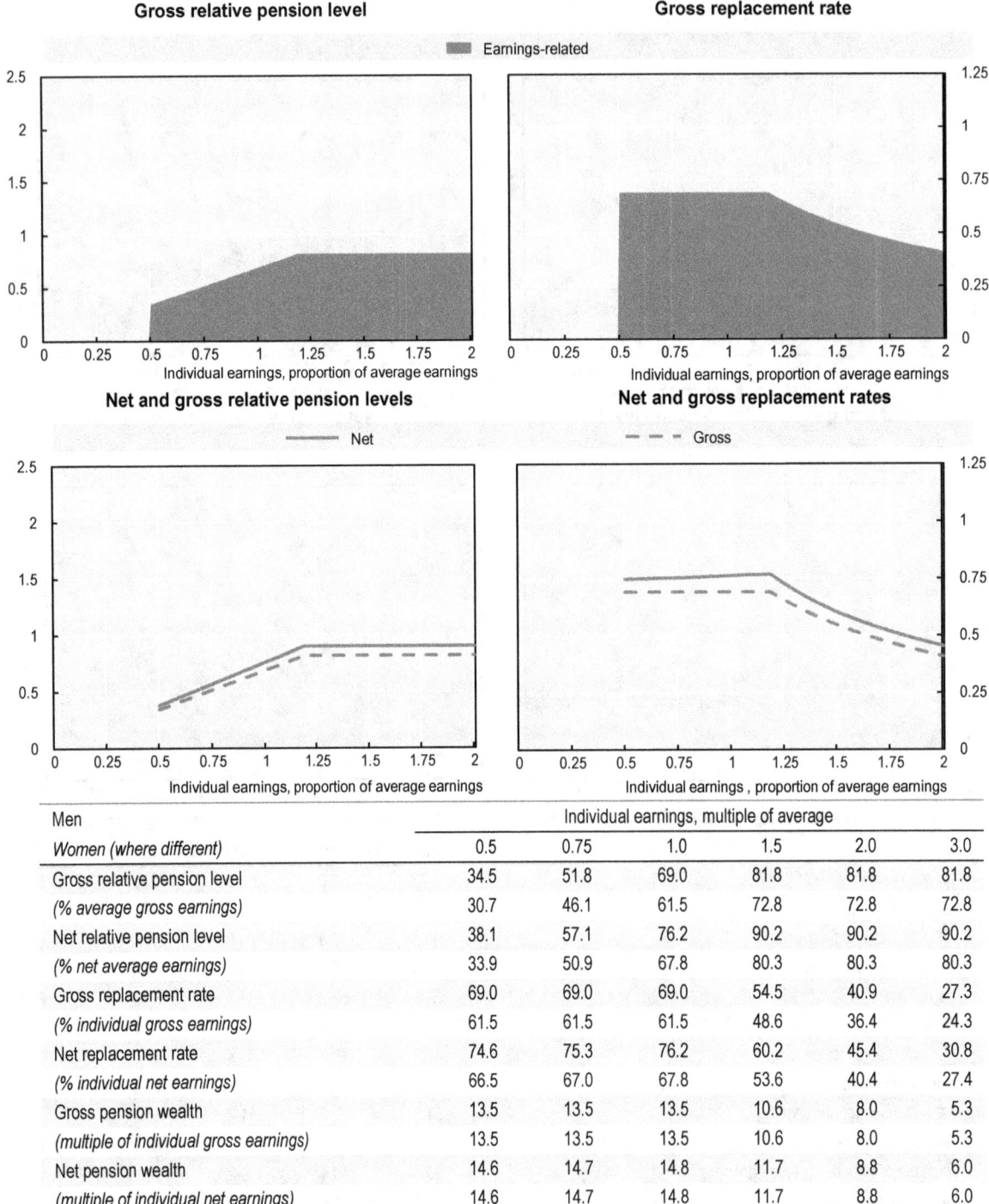

Men	Individual earnings, multiple of average					
Women (where different)	0.5	0.75	1.0	1.5	2.0	3.0
Gross relative pension level	34.5	51.8	69.0	81.8	81.8	81.8
(% average gross earnings)	30.7	46.1	61.5	72.8	72.8	72.8
Net relative pension level	38.1	57.1	76.2	90.2	90.2	90.2
(% net average earnings)	33.9	50.9	67.8	80.3	80.3	80.3
Gross replacement rate	69.0	69.0	69.0	54.5	40.9	27.3
(% individual gross earnings)	61.5	61.5	61.5	48.6	36.4	24.3
Net replacement rate	74.6	75.3	76.2	60.2	45.4	30.8
(% individual net earnings)	66.5	67.0	67.8	53.6	40.4	27.4
Gross pension wealth	13.5	13.5	13.5	10.6	8.0	5.3
(multiple of individual gross earnings)	13.5	13.5	13.5	10.6	8.0	5.3
Net pension wealth	14.6	14.7	14.8	11.7	8.8	6.0
(multiple of individual net earnings)	14.6	14.7	14.8	11.7	8.8	6.0

Assumptions: Real rate of return 3%, real earnings growth 1.25%, inflation 2%, and real discount rate 2%. All systems are modelled and indexed according to what is legislated. Transitional rules apply where relevant. DC conversion rate equal 90%. Labour market entry occurs at age 20 in 2016. Tax system latest available: 2016.

StatLink http://dx.doi.org/10.1787/888933873820

Sri Lanka

Sri Lanka: Pension system in 2016.

Employees in the formal private sector are covered by defined contribution plans: Employees Provident Fund, which is used in the model, Employees Trust Fund or approved private sector provident fund. Civil servants were formally covered by public sector pension scheme.

Key indicators: Sri Lanka

		Sri Lanka	OECD
Average earnings	LKR	300 000	5 436 183
	USD	2 021	36 622
Public pension spending	% of GDP	1.4	8.2
Life expectancy	at birth	75.6	80.9
	at age 65	17.1	19.7
Population over age 65	% of working-age population	14.1	23.4

StatLink http://dx.doi.org/10.1787/888933873839

Qualifying conditions

At age 55 for men and 50 for women.

Benefit calculation

Defined contribution

Employee's provident fund is a fully funded defined-contribution plan and employees contribute 8% of wage and employers pay 12%. The entire lump sum, including interest, is paid at the time of exit. The annual interest rate must be at least 2.5%. For comparison with other economies, for replacement rate purposes the pension is shown as a price-indexed annuity based on sex-specific mortality rates.

Variant careers

Early retirement

At any age if the government closes the place of employment, if emigrating permanently, or for employed women who marry.

Late retirement

It is not possible to start claiming pension after the normal pension age.

Personal income tax and social security contributions

Taxation of workers

There is no income tax relief and the deduction of work-related expenses.

Taxation of worker's income

Annual income band	Tax rate
Up to LKR 500 000	4%
LKR 500 001- LKR 1 000 000	8%
LKR 1 000 001- LKR 1 500 000	12%
LKR 1 500 001 – LKR 2 000 000	16%
LKR 2 000 001 – LKR 3 000 000	20%
Over LKR 3 000 000	24%

Social security contributions payable by workers

Employees' contributions are deductible up to a limit of LKR 25 000 per annum.

Taxation of pensioners

All purchased annuities of retirees are exempt.

Taxation of pension income

Annual income band	Tax rate
Up to LKR 2 000 000	0
LKR 2 000 001- LKR 2 500 000	5%
LKR 2 500 001- LKR 3 000 000	10%
Over LKR 3 000 000	15%

Social security contributions payable by pensioners

Pensioners do not pay any social security contributions.

Pension modelling results: Sri Lanka in 2051 retirement at age 55 (men)

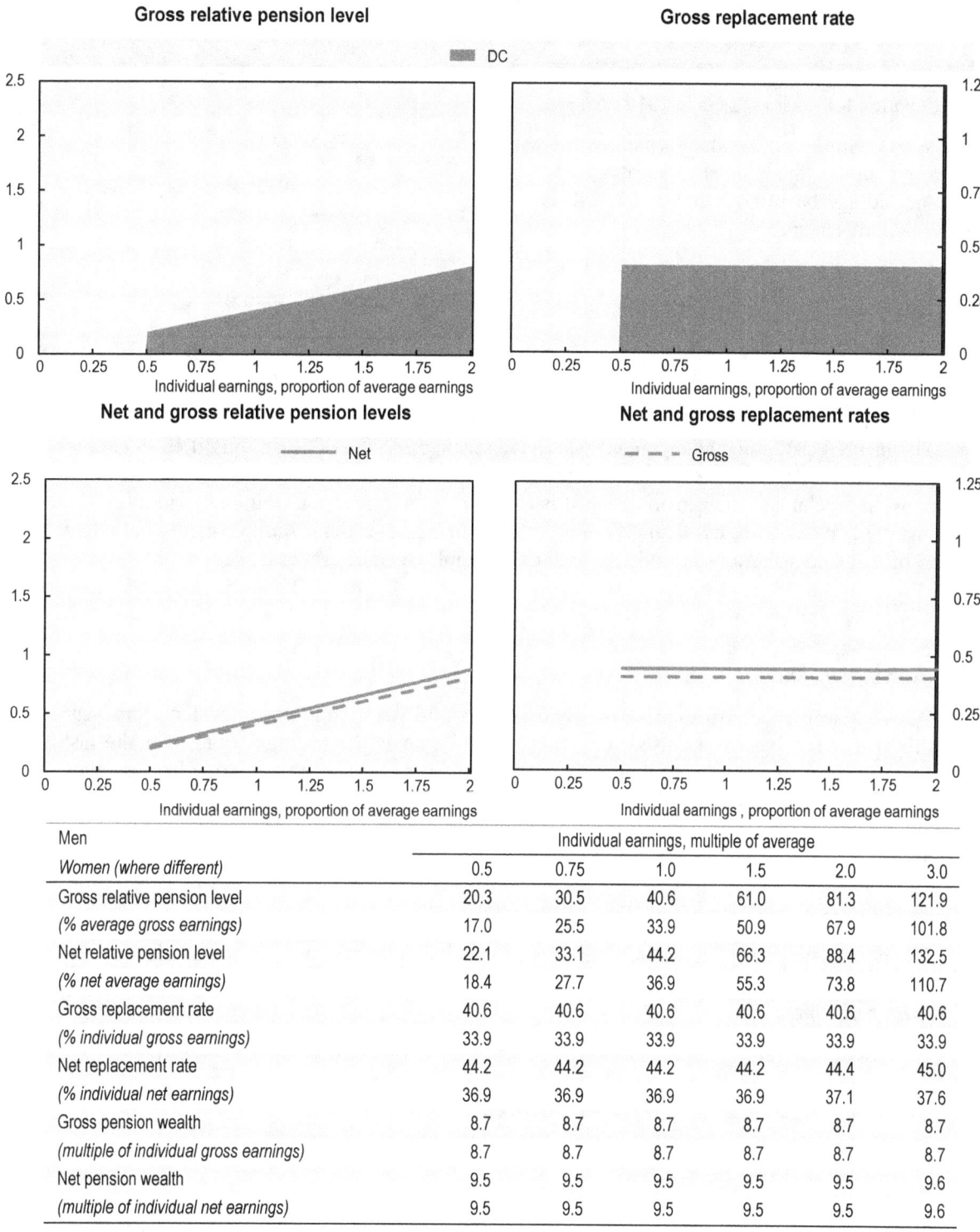

Men	Individual earnings, multiple of average					
Women (where different)	0.5	0.75	1.0	1.5	2.0	3.0
Gross relative pension level	20.3	30.5	40.6	61.0	81.3	121.9
(% average gross earnings)	17.0	25.5	33.9	50.9	67.9	101.8
Net relative pension level	22.1	33.1	44.2	66.3	88.4	132.5
(% net average earnings)	18.4	27.7	36.9	55.3	73.8	110.7
Gross replacement rate	40.6	40.6	40.6	40.6	40.6	40.6
(% individual gross earnings)	33.9	33.9	33.9	33.9	33.9	33.9
Net replacement rate	44.2	44.2	44.2	44.2	44.4	45.0
(% individual net earnings)	36.9	36.9	36.9	36.9	37.1	37.6
Gross pension wealth	8.7	8.7	8.7	8.7	8.7	8.7
(multiple of individual gross earnings)	8.7	8.7	8.7	8.7	8.7	8.7
Net pension wealth	9.5	9.5	9.5	9.5	9.5	9.6
(multiple of individual net earnings)	9.5	9.5	9.5	9.5	9.5	9.6

Assumptions: Real rate of return 3%, real earnings growth 1.25%, inflation 2%, and real discount rate 2%. All systems are modelled and indexed according to what is legislated. Transitional rules apply where relevant. DC conversion rate equal 90%. Labour market entry occurs at age 20 in 2016. Tax system latest available: 2016.

StatLink http://dx.doi.org/10.1787/888933873858

Thailand

Thailand: Pension system in 2016

Private sector employees in the formal sectors are covered under the Social Security Fund (SSF). The old-age benefit scheme under SSF is a defined benefit scheme.

Key indicators: Thailand

		Thailand	OECD
Average earnings	THB	174 319	1 311 437
	USD	4 868	36 622
Public pension spending	% of GDP	2.4	8.2
Life expectancy	at birth	75.6	80.9
	at age 65	18.3	19.7
Population over age 65	% of working-age population	14.8	23.4

StatLink http://dx.doi.org/10.1787/888933873877

Qualifying conditions

The insured (both men and women) who have reached the age of 55 are qualified to get old age benefit. At least 180 months (15 years) of contributions are required for monthly pension receipt and the pension benefit is adjusted for a longer contribution period. For the insured persons with less than 180 months of contribution a lump sum payment equivalent to the total contributions is made. In both cases employment must cease.

Benefit calculation

Earnings-related

Workers accrue 20% of their earnings for the first 15 years and then 1.5% for every year thereafter. The base wage used for benefit calculation is the average wage over the last five years prior to retirement. Indexation rules are discretionary and the modelling assumes price indexation of pensions in payment.

Variant careers

Early retirement

It is not possible to claim the earnings-related pension before the normal age of 55.

Late retirement

It is possible to retire later than the age of 55 and the pension continues to accrue by 1.5%.

Personal income tax and social security contributions

Taxation of workers

There are various tax relief systems and the employed receive a tax deduction of 50% of assessable income up to THB 100 000. Single insured persons receive a personal allowance of THB 60 000. Social security contributions are tax deductible.

Taxation of worker's income

Annual taxable income	Tax rate
1-THB 150 000	0%
THB 150 001-THB 300 000	5%
THB 300 001-THB 500 000	10%
THB 500 001-THB 750 000	15%
THB 750 001-THB 1 000 000	20%
THB 1 000 001-THB 2 000 000	25%
THB 2 000 001-THB 5 000 000	30%
THB 5 000 001 and over	35%

Social security contributions payable by workers

Insured persons pay social security contributions. For old age pension, the contribution rate is 3% between the floor of THB 1 650 per month and the ceiling of THB 15 000 per month. They also pay 1.5% of earnings for sickness, maternity, invalidity and death benefits and 0.5% of earnings for the unemployment insurance scheme.

Taxation of pensioners

All pension incomes are exempted from taxation. The elderly above 65 who continue working receive an old age tax allowance of THB 190 000.

Social security contributions payable by pensioners

Pensioners do not pay any social security contributions.

Pension modelling results: Thailand in 2051 retirement at age 55

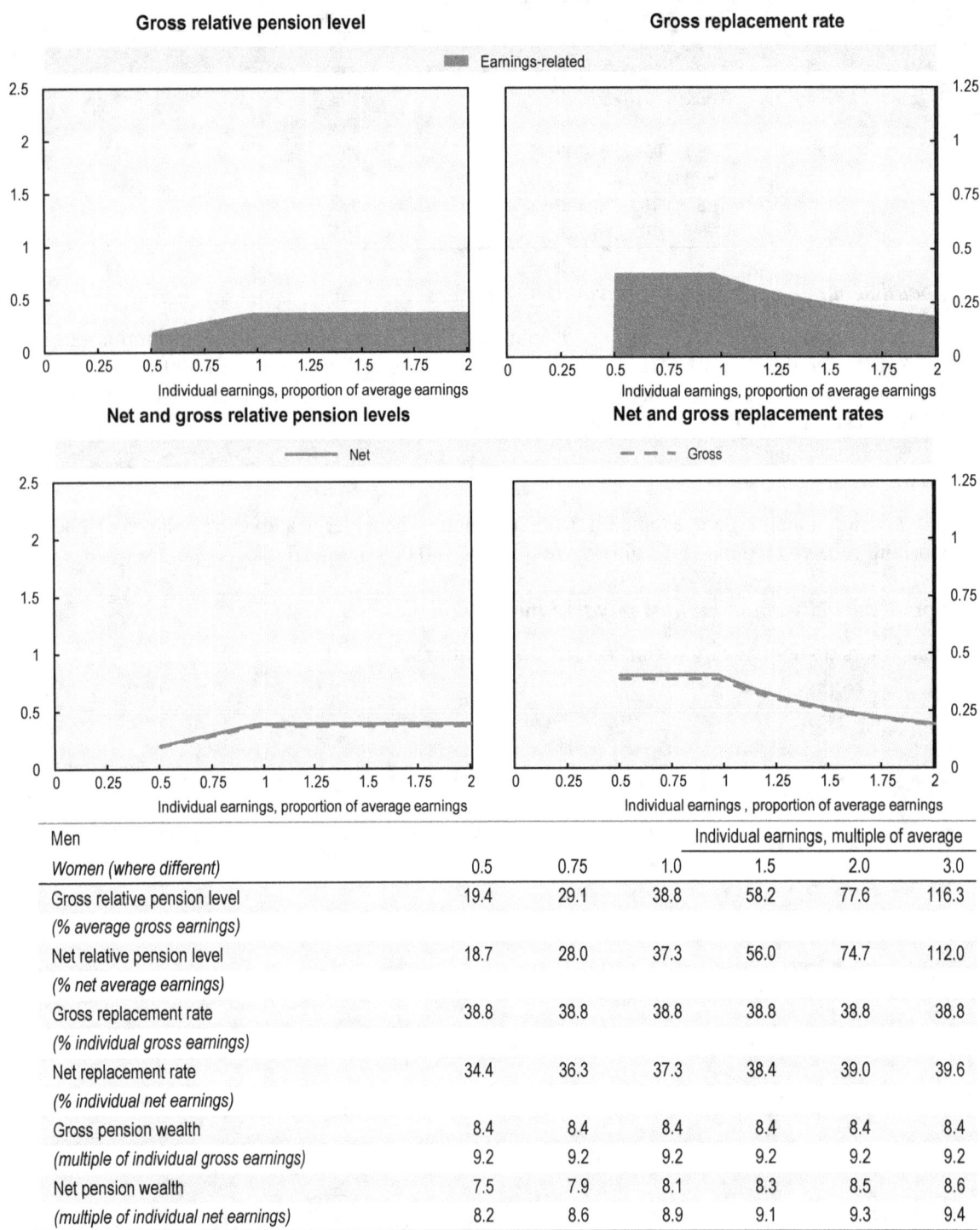

Men						
				Individual earnings, multiple of average		
Women (where different)	0.5	0.75	1.0	1.5	2.0	3.0
Gross relative pension level	19.4	29.1	38.8	58.2	77.6	116.3
(% average gross earnings)						
Net relative pension level	18.7	28.0	37.3	56.0	74.7	112.0
(% net average earnings)						
Gross replacement rate	38.8	38.8	38.8	38.8	38.8	38.8
(% individual gross earnings)						
Net replacement rate	34.4	36.3	37.3	38.4	39.0	39.6
(% individual net earnings)						
Gross pension wealth	8.4	8.4	8.4	8.4	8.4	8.4
(multiple of individual gross earnings)	9.2	9.2	9.2	9.2	9.2	9.2
Net pension wealth	7.5	7.9	8.1	8.3	8.5	8.6
(multiple of individual net earnings)	8.2	8.6	8.9	9.1	9.3	9.4

Assumptions: Real rate of return 3%, real earnings growth 1.25%, inflation 2%, and real discount rate 2%. All systems are modelled and indexed according to what is legislated. Transitional rules apply where relevant. DC conversion rate equal 90%. Labour market entry occurs at age 20 in 2016. Tax system latest available: 2016.

StatLink http://dx.doi.org/10.1787/888933873896

Viet Nam

Viet Nam: Pension system in 2016

Viet Nam Social Security (VSS) manages and administers social security contributions and benefits (including pensions) for both private sector workers and government workers. The current pension scheme is a pay-as-you-go defined benefit (PAYG DB) scheme.

Key indicators: Viet Nam

		Viet Nam	OECD
Average earnings	VND (million)	46.1	833.8
	USD	2 025	36 622
Public pension spending	% of GDP	2.7	8.2
Life expectancy	at birth	76.5	80.9
	at age 65	18.7	19.7
Population over age 65	% of working-age population	9.6	23.4

StatLink http://dx.doi.org/10.1787/888933873915

Qualifying conditions

Normal pension age is 60 for men and 55 for women with a minimum of 20 years of contributions. A lump sum payment is made for people with shorter contribution periods.

Benefit calculation

Earnings-related

For the first 15 years of contribution, the pension accrual rate is 3% for both males and females, and then is 2% for males and 3% for females for each additional year. Between 2018 and 2022 the number of years will increase to 20 for men and from 2018 the additional accrual for women will be lowered to 2%. The maximum replacement rate is 75% of the insured's average earnings.

Old-age grant

If total contributions are less than 20 years, retirees receive a lump sum is paid of 1.5 times the insured's covered average monthly earnings in the last five years for years of contributions before 2014, plus 2 times the insured's covered average monthly earnings in the last five years for contributions since 2014.

Old-age social assistance

According to the Decree 136/2013/NĐ-CP dated 21 October 2013, a minimum social pension is VND 270 000. A multiplier is applied with this minimum level: (i) 1.5 (or benefit is VND 405 000) for those aged 60 to 79 who are living in poor households without family members, or with support from family members who are also receiving social assistance benefits; (ii) 2 (or benefit is VND 540 000) for those aged 80 and over who are living in poor households without family members, or with support from family members who are also receiving social assistance benefits; and 1 (or benefit is VND 270 000) for those aged 80 and over who do not have any social insurance and assistance benefits; and (iii) 3 (or benefit is VND 810 000) for any older people who are living in poor households without family members but receiving support from community.

Variant careers

Early retirement

It is possible to retire and to start claiming the pension at age 55 for men and 50 for women under specific requirements. The pension is reduced by 2% of the insured's covered average monthly earnings for each year the pension is taken before the insured's normal pensionable age due to reduced working capacity.

Late retirement

It is not possible to start claiming a pension after the normal pension age. It is possible, however, to combine working and receiving pension.

Personal income tax and social security contributions

Taxation of workers

There is a personal allowance of VND 9 million per month.

Taxation of worker's income

Tax rates applicable to regular annual income are as follows:

Taxed income per year	Tax rate
Up to VND 60 000 000	5%
From VND 60 000 000 up to VND 120 000 000	10%
From VND 120 000 000 up to VND 216 000 000	15%
From VND 216 000 000 up to VND 384 000 000	20%
From VND 384 000 000 up to VND 624 000 000	25%
From VND 624 000 000 up to VND 960 000 000	30%
From VND 960 000 000	35%

Social security contributions payable by workers

Employees pay 8% of monthly salary/wage for retirement benefits. The minimum and maximum monthly earnings for contribution and benefit calculation purposes are the minimum wage and 20 times of the minimum wage, respectively. As such, for 1 July 2017 – 1 July 2018, they are VND 1 300 000 and VND 26 000 000, respectively; and for 1 July 2018 onwards they will be VND 1 390 000 and VND 27 800 000, respectively.

Taxation of pensioners

There is no additional tax relief for pensioners.

Taxation of pension income

The same taxation rule is applied to pension benefits.

Social security contributions payable by pensioners

Pensioners do not pay any social security contributions.

Pension modelling results: Viet Nam in 2056 retirement at age 60 (men)

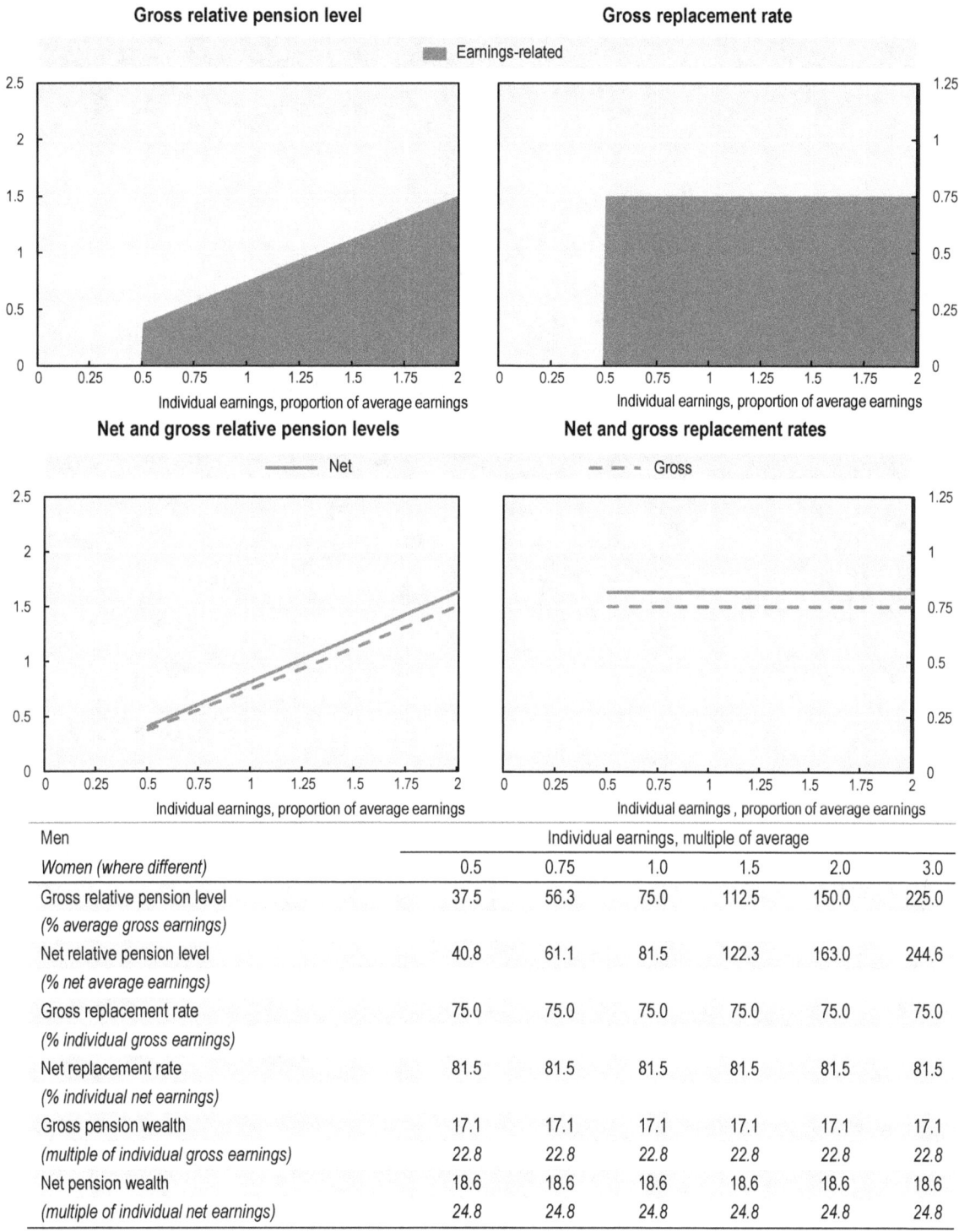

Men	Individual earnings, multiple of average					
Women (where different)	0.5	0.75	1.0	1.5	2.0	3.0
Gross relative pension level	37.5	56.3	75.0	112.5	150.0	225.0
(% average gross earnings)						
Net relative pension level	40.8	61.1	81.5	122.3	163.0	244.6
(% net average earnings)						
Gross replacement rate	75.0	75.0	75.0	75.0	75.0	75.0
(% individual gross earnings)						
Net replacement rate	81.5	81.5	81.5	81.5	81.5	81.5
(% individual net earnings)						
Gross pension wealth	17.1	17.1	17.1	17.1	17.1	17.1
(multiple of individual gross earnings)	22.8	22.8	22.8	22.8	22.8	22.8
Net pension wealth	18.6	18.6	18.6	18.6	18.6	18.6
(multiple of individual net earnings)	24.8	24.8	24.8	24.8	24.8	24.8

Assumptions: Real rate of return 3%, real earnings growth 1.25%, inflation 2%, and real discount rate 2%. All systems are modelled and indexed according to what is legislated. Transitional rules apply where relevant. DC conversion rate equal 90%. Labour market entry occurs at age 20 in 2016. Tax system latest available: 2016.

StatLink http://dx.doi.org/10.1787/888933873934

ORGANISATION FOR ECONOMIC CO-OPERATION AND DEVELOPMENT

The OECD is a unique forum where governments work together to address the economic, social and environmental challenges of globalisation. The OECD is also at the forefront of efforts to understand and to help governments respond to new developments and concerns, such as corporate governance, the information economy and the challenges of an ageing population. The Organisation provides a setting where governments can compare policy experiences, seek answers to common problems, identify good practice and work to co-ordinate domestic and international policies.

The OECD member countries are: Australia, Austria, Belgium, Canada, Chile, the Czech Republic, Denmark, Estonia, Finland, France, Germany, Greece, Hungary, Iceland, Ireland, Israel, Italy, Japan, Korea, Latvia, Lithuania, Luxembourg, Mexico, the Netherlands, New Zealand, Norway, Poland, Portugal, the Slovak Republic, Slovenia, Spain, Sweden, Switzerland, Turkey, the United Kingdom and the United States. The European Union takes part in the work of the OECD.

OECD Publishing disseminates widely the results of the Organisation's statistics gathering and research on economic, social and environmental issues, as well as the conventions, guidelines and standards agreed by its members.

OECD PUBLISHING, 2, rue André-Pascal, 75775 PARIS CEDEX 16
(81 2018 18 1 P) ISBN 978-92-64-30868-8 – 2018

www.ingramcontent.com/pod-product-compliance
Lightning Source LLC
Chambersburg PA
CBHW082358220526
45470CB00008B/2783